UNIVERSITY OF NORTH CAROLINA AT CHAPEL HILL
DEPARTMENT OF ROMANCE LANGUAGES

NORTH CAROLINA STUDIES
IN THE ROMANCE LANGUAGES AND LITERATURES

Founder: URBAN TIGNER HOLMES

Distributed by:

UNIVERSITY OF NORTH CAROLINA PRESS

CHAPEL HILL

North Carolina 27514

U.S.A.

NORTH CAROLINA STUDIES IN THE
ROMANCE LANGUAGES AND LITERATURES
Number 195

SANTIAGO F. PUGLIA,

AN EARLY PHILADELPHIA PROPAGANDIST
FOR SPANISH AMERICAN INDEPENDENCE

SANTIAGO F. PUGLIA,

AN EARLY PHILADELPHIA PROPAGANDIST FOR SPANISH AMERICAN INDEPENDENCE

BY

MERLE E. SIMMONS

CHAPEL HILL

NORTH CAROLINA STUDIES IN THE
ROMANCE LANGUAGES AND LITERATURES
U.N.C. DEPARTMENT OF ROMANCE LANGUAGES

1977

Library of Congress Cataloging in Publication Data

Simmons, Merle Edwin, 1918-
  Santiago F. Puglia, an early Philadelphia propagandist for Spanish American independence.

  (North Carolina studies in the Romance languages and literatures; no. 195)
  Bibliography: p.
  1. Puglia, James Philip. El desengaño del hombre. 2. Puglia, James Philip
— Bibliography. 3. Latin America — History — To 1830. I. Title. II. Series.

JC186.P83S55   320.5'092'4   77-21532
ISBN 0-8078-9195-9

I.S.B.N. 0-8078-9195-9

DEPÓSITO LEGAL: V. 2.909 - 1977   I.S.B.N. 84-399-7593-7
ARTES GRÁFICAS SOLER, S. A. - JÁVEA, 28 - VALENCIA (8) - 1977

TABLE OF CONTENTS

	Page
PREFACE	9

CHAPTER

		Page
I.	Puglia's Biography, 1760-1794	13
II.	The Contents of *El desengaño del hombre*	25
III.	*El desengaño del hombre* in the Spanish World	41
IV.	More on Puglia's Biography, 1794-1822	49
V.	Puglia's Publications in Spanish in 1821-1822	55
VI.	Other Works in English and Unpublished Manuscripts	62
VII.	Epilogue	65

	Page
BIBLIOGRAPHY OF THE WORKS OF SANTIAGO F. PUGLIA	74

PREFACE

When Santiago F. Puglia came down the gangplank at Philadelphia on July 22, 1790, forty-eight days out of Cádiz on the ship Aurora, he brought with him as part of his intellectual baggage a mind full of French libertarian ideas and a fecund hatred of the Spanish monarchical government and the Spanish Church. Puglia's anti-Spanish spleen was to produce within the space of some thirty months a furibund attack upon the whole governmental, religious, and colonial system of Spain. *El desengaño del hombre* he entitled the small but deadly political tirade that he issued in Philadelphia in early 1794. Not since Bartolomé de las Casas had wielded a pen dipped in vitriol and moral fervor had any other printed book, treatise, or essay in any language made such a frontal attack on Spain and the very foundations of its colonial empire in America. Puglia's aim was immodest —no less than to revolutionize Spain and her empire—and although his campaign was premature and therefore doomed to be disappointing, there can be little doubt that he succeeded for a brief moment in agitating Spanish colonial administrators both in Spain and America to a degree that they had probably not experienced for well over two centuries, at least not as a consequence of the printed word.

Puglia's little book is all but unknown to both historians and literary scholars. Though its publication is contemporary with Antonio Nariño's translation of the French *Droits de l'homme* in Bogotá and antedates by several years the famous *Carta a los españoles americanos* of the Peruvian Jesuit, Juan Pablo Viscardo y Guzmán, Puglia's work has seldom received more than passing mention in histories of Spanish American independence, studies of the Spanish and Spanish American Enlightenment, or histories of Spanish American literature.

Recently three tentative exploratory articles have appeared,[1] but Puglia still remains little more than a name to most Hispanists. I propose to remedy this situation, at least partially, by offering here the results of some recent efforts of my own to learn more about Puglia and his works. Actually, *El desengaño del hombre*, though undoubtedly the most interesting of his politico-literary efforts, is only the first of several books and translations in both Spanish and English that Puglia bequeathed to the world. Its second edition in 1822, a Spanish translation of Tom Paine's *Rights of Man*, one other political work in Spanish, and some four or five books and pamphlets written in English attest to Puglia's activity as an early purveyor of democratic ideas.

★ ★ ★

My research, beyond what I have been able to do in the Indiana University Library, has been carried on almost exclusively in the Library of Congress and in several libraries in Philadelphia. I am well aware that a great deal more could probably be learned about Puglia in at least five other locales: Italy, his birthplace; Spain, particularly Cádiz, where he spent about five years of his early manhood; Mexico, where one of his brothers lived and where Spanish officials reacted with alarm to the publication of his book; Harrisburg, Pennsylvania, his place of residence from about 1802 to 1805; and Charleston, South Carolina, where he died. Although I have not been able to visit these places in order to exhaust my subject, the time has come, I believe, to make available the results of my investigations up to this point in the hope that other scholars may be moved to look into

---

[1] Lucía Fox, "Dos precursores de la independencia hispanoamericana y sus obras editadas en Filadelfia entre 1794 y 1799," *Interamerican Review of Bibliography* [*Revista Interamericana de Bibliografía*] (Washington, D. C.), XIX (1969), 407-414; also, "Un documento ignorado en el movimiento de emancipación americana," *Razón y Fábula* (Bogotá, Colombia), No. 31 (enero-marzo, 1973), 13-32; and A. Owen Aldridge, "A Spanish Precursor of *The Age of Reason*," in *Papers on French-Spanish, Luso-Brazilian, Spanish-American Literary Relations, Discussed at Conference 8, Modern Language Association of America, New York, December, 1968*, ed. by Marie A. Wellington (Elmhurst, Illinois: Spanish Department, Elmhurst College, n. d. [1969?]), pp. 1-4. The earliest significant mention of Puglia that I am aware of is in Jefferson Rea Spell's *Rousseau in the Spanish World before 1833* (Austin: University of Texas Press, 1938), pp. 220-221. Jean Sarrailh in *La España ilustrada de la segunda mitad del siglo XVIII* (México-Buenos Aires: Fondo de Cultura Económica, 1957) accords Puglia one brief paragraph (p. 577), but he believed that Puglia was a Mexican.

aspects of Puglia's life and writings that I have not been able to explore.

Because mine is an introductory study, and because until very recently when the Library of Congress issued a photocopied edition of *El desengaño del hombre*, Puglia's main book could be read only in a handful of libraries, I have elected to include in Chapter II a fairly detailed summary of the work's contents for the benefit of those readers — surely a substantial majority — who have not seen the book and even yet do not have a copy of it readily available. I feel constrained to note, however, that my summary is quite long, heavily laden with quoted passages, and perhaps a bit wearisome. To any readers who are disposed to accept on faith that Puglia's assault on Spain's government and his call to rebellion were indeed heady stuff for their time, I say now that they may prefer to skim this chapter lightly, though I hasten to add that by so doing they may fail to learn as much about Puglia, the author and the man, as they might wish. Precisely because the rarity of Puglia's book has made it all but impossible for most readers to know either the work or its author, my method here has been to let the writer speak for himself and, by giving readers a fairly detailed summary of his ideas and citing generous samples of his prose, to provide them an opportunity to form their own impressions of his personality, modes of thought, and literary style. It is appropriate in this connection that I apprise my readers also of the fact that all quotations cited from Puglia's works are here reproduced exactly as they appear, and in the case of *El desengaño del hombre* all quoted passages are from the 1794 edition. Obvious errors of style, spelling, and grammar and Puglia's highly personal punctuation are all faithfully reproduced because I believe that my readers will want to savor the picturesque and extremely colorful prose of a frequently incorrect but always irrepressible writer. The only exceptions to this procedure are corrections that I have made in accordance with a list of *Erratas* that Puglia himself placed at the beginning of *El desengaño del hombre*.

CHAPTER I

PUGLIA'S BIOGRAPHY, 1760-1794

Most of what we know of Santiago Felipe Puglia's life comes from the author himself. In part because of a certain egocentrism and in part because of a desire to make known to the world at large the existence of numerous unpublished manuscripts of various kinds which he hoped would attract the attention of some friendly printer, Puglia was wont to append to almost all of his published books *adiciones* or appendices that contained, in addition to the titles of such unpublished works, occasional biographical details about himself and his personal problems, particularly the poverty and misfortune that plagued him throughout his life in the United States. From these come the woof and warp of the data that we have about his biography, though many other details, minor for the most part but frequently illuminating, have come to light from my examination of newspapers, manuscript collections, and other, sometimes unlikely, sources.

In a lengthy *adición* to *El desengaño del hombre*, the author himself makes his introduction into the literary and political world with a footnote that reads as follows:

> Nació el Autor de esta obra el dia 1° de Mayo 1760 en Génova Ciudad Capital y República Aristocrática. Fué bautizado el mismo dia en la Iglesia Parroquial y Colegiada de SANTA MARIA de las Viñas. Su Padre Juan Domingo, del Comercio de dicha Ciudad, es natural de la Prefectura de Blenio jurisdiccion de los tres Cantones Suizos, Uri, Switz y Underwalden. Sentiria muchísimo el Autor de que alguno le creyese ambicioso en decir que es Genovés; muy al contrario, siendo su único objeto de provar que no es Español. Un alma que tiene democrática disposición niega y aborrece su

Patria, si tiene otro Gobierno menos del popular. Pésale desde luego de haber nacido en Génova, y de tal casualidad sus padres tienen la culpa; siendo así que otra Patria no conoce para si, sino la Tierra en donde reyna la verdadera Libertad, segun decia el inmortal Doctor Franklin.[1] (p. iv)

Proud of his family, which he claims counted among its number some men "who have filled at different periods some of the important offices of that Government [i. e., the cantons of Uri, Schwyz, and Unterwalden]," Puglia also was grateful to his father for having provided his sons an opportunity to travel as part of their early education.[2] Then, from 1775-1782 the young Swiss-Italian studied at the College of Savona, thirty miles west of Genoa,[3] where he claimed to have completed a regular course in Theology.[4]

Five years later, in 1787, Puglia, following in the footsteps of his father, was established as a successful merchant in Cádiz and was fighting a losing battle against Spanish injustice:

El Autor fué Comerciante en la Ciudad y Plaza de Cádiz. Por atrazos improvisos é irremediables quebró el año 87. Refugióse en la Iglesia y fué sacado de ella; padeció 18 meses de prision en la carcel de dicha Ciudad, y así que la inhumanidad de un codicioso é injusto Acreedor vióse cansada, decretósele libertad en Marzo de 89. Pobre y desvalido aprovechóse de su antigua amistad con un Capitan Americano, quien le traxo gratuitamente á esta en donde llegó el dia 22 de Julio 1790, y empezó á buscar su vida enseñando la lengua Castellana. Parecen increibles los procedimientos del

---

[1] (Filadelfia: En la imprenta de Francisco Bailey, 1794). Despite Puglia's humorously vehement rejection of any kind of personal ties with an undemocratic Spain, a perceptive reader cannot fail to note that in all of his books written *in Spanish* this resolute defender of democratic ideas seeks clearly to identify himself with Hispanic culture, perhaps in order to cultivate an emotional tie with his Spanish readers, by always signing himself with the very Spanish names of Santiago Felipe. When writing in English he calls himself James Philip or uses the pseudonym of James Quicksilver, and at the end of his life, for reasons not presently known, he apparently was using the French form of his name, Jacques Philip (see p. 69 below).

[2] James Ph. Puglia, *The Federal Politician* (Philadelphia: Printed by Francis & Robert Bailey, 1795), p. 62.

[3] Ibid., p. 82.

[4] "Having finished a regular course of Theology, I think myself at least, as equally entitled to speak occasionally on religious topics as those living fanatics, who have of *late* become Deists...." Ibid., p. 198.

Fuero Español en esa parte, sin embargo es un facto constante. Los Autos que yacen entregados al polvo y olvido en la Escribania del Consulado de Cadiz, pueden ser en todo tiempo la prueva auténtica de lo que esta lacónica narracion contiene. Déxanse en silencio las nulidades que se cometiéron en el principio y decurso de ellos, como tambien las opresiones y trabajos que el infeliz pacientemente toleró, pues alguno pensaria que estos escritos procedan de un ánimo vengativo. Dios perdone al juez, escribano, perseguidor, y en particular al Juzgado Eclesiástico, el qual por materia de algun secreto galardon vendió los privilegios del sagrado, quebrantó la fe de hospitalidad, y consintió un atropellamiento tan escandaloso y sin exemplar.[5] (pp. x-xi)

How Puglia managed to live for over a year in Cádiz from the time of his release from jail in March, 1789, until he embarked for the United States on June 4, 1790,[6] can only be conjectured at the present time. That he probably did not leave Cádiz during this period is to be inferred from a statement wherein he refers to a tax measure that was issued "en el principio del año 90 (estando el Autor en Cádiz)...." (p. 23)

Having reached Philadelphia, Puglia spent the next two years of his life in obscurity. In May, 1791, he took the oath of allegiance as a naturalized citizen of the United States[7] at a time when he presumably was quietly earning a modest livelihood as a teacher of Spanish and perhaps working as a bookkeeper;[8] at least by late 1792 he was so

---

[5] Many years later Puglia recalls the same events and adds that he came "... to this land of liberty, with the avowed purpose of exposing the sceptre of despotism to the world and particularly to the South American colonies." James Ph. Puglia, *Forgery Defeated; or A New Plan for Invalidating and Detecting All Attempts of the Kind; for Which a Patent Has Been Obtained from the United States* (Philadelphia: J. F. Hurtel, 1822), pp. 21-22.

[6] Puglia does not reveal the date of his departure from Cádiz or the name of the ship on which he traveled. As noted above, however, he states that he arrived in Philadelphia on July 22, 1790. On July 30, the *Pennsylvania Packet and Daily Advertiser* of Philadelphia printed a news item about war in Spain brought "by the ship Aurora, arrived at Philadelphia on Friday last from Cádiz, which she left on the 4th of June...." Friday actually was July 23, but it is not improbable that the arrival occurred late on Thursday, July 22, thus causing a slight discrepancy in the two accounts.

[7] *Federal Politician*, p. 153.

[8] In several numbers of the *Pennsylvania Packet and Daily Advertiser* beginning with that of December 14, 1790, an advertisement appears that reads as follows:

employed in a business house engaged in international trade.[9] Then in August of 1792 his fortune and his prestige improved significantly when he was officially commissioned Interpreter of the Spanish Language for the Commonwealth of Pennsylvania.[10] Not without importance is the fact that the lonely exile from European despotism had thus moved, albeit on a humble level, into the official family of Governor Thomas Mifflin[11] toward whom Pennsylvania radicals were gravitating during the early years of the 1790's when the tugging and hauling between Federalists and Republicans was giving rise to the formation of a party system in the United States.[12]

By January, 1793, Puglia's mind and his energies were being increasingly occupied by a project which he no doubt had been contemplating from the day he made his decision to leave Spain and come to America, and on January 14, 1793, he resigned his bookkeeping job in order to devote more time to writing a book in Spanish. Let the author describe his state of mind and his problems in his own words:

SPANISH LANGUAGE

James Ph. D. de Puglia, takes the liberty of informing the public that in consequence of his having dissolved partnership with those with whom he was at first engaged, he has moved from Videll's Alley, to Front street above Arch street, at No. 77, where he intends to teach the *Spanish language*... [etc.].

It is possible, of course, that the partnership referred to above was other than a teaching enterprise. The reference may be to some kind of business activity, perhaps one in which Puglia drew upon his experience in commerce with Spain.

[9] See below, p. 10.

[10] In *El desengaño del hombre* (p. xiv) Puglia says that he received his appointment on August 25. The Executive Minutes of Governor Thomas Mifflin (*Pennsylvania Archives*, 9th Series, Vol. I [n. p.: Bureau of Publications, 1931], p. 438) state that the commission was given on August 23.

[11] In later years Puglia wrote Thomas Jefferson that "If you recollect my occasional services in your office, as Interpreter, during the years 1792 & 1793, my name will be remembered by you." Letter from Puglia to Jefferson dated Philadelphia, June 21, 1808, in E. Millicent Sowerby, comp., *Catalogue of the Library of Thomas Jefferson* (Washington, D. C.: The Library of Congress), IV, 557. The original is in the Jefferson Papers in the Manuscript Division of the Library of Congress. Since Puglia refers here to "occasional" services, it is probable that Governor Mifflin shared his official interpreter with Jefferson, then Secretary of State, whenever his services were needed.

[12] See W. O. Lynch, *Fifty Years of Party Warfare, 1789-1837* (Indianapolis: Bobbs-Merrill Co., 1931); Eugene Perry Link, *Democratic-Republican Societies, 1790-1800* (Morningside Heights, N. Y.: Columbia University

Quando emprendí esta tarea tenia bastantes discipulos, y á demas el empleo de tenedor de libros en una Casa de Comercio respetable en este Continente, y en las demas partes del Globo; ambas faenas tenian sus horas destinadas sin interrupcion, y puedo afirmar que vivia ocupado y contento. Seguí la empresa algun tiempo sin faltar á mis diarias obligaciones, pero iba muy de espacio en ella. La priesa que me hacian los Amigos de la libertad para su remate, infundia ánimo á mi trabajo, pues todos á una voz me profetizaban una favorable aceptación. (pp. vi-vii)

Puglia goes on to explain that he wrote to the French government and also to Thomas Paine seeking help in publishing his projected book, but that in the absence of any kind of reply he made the personal sacrifice of giving up his bookkeeping job on January 14, 1793, in order to devote more of his time to his writing.

To be noted here are several significant details. Puglia's reference to the "Amigos de la libertad" I shall deal with at some length below, but no less arresting are, first, his effort to obtain assistance from the revolutionary government of France, and, second, his approach to Tom Paine, then a deputy in the French Convention, which reveals, I suspect, Puglia's instinctive association of his own advanced ideas with the English-American pamphleteer's flaming brand of political radicalism. In this connection it should be borne in mind that Puglia's enduring admiration for Paine was to bear fruit not only in *El desengaño del hombre*, wherein he translated a few pages of *The Rights of Man*, thus offering the world its first translation of Paine in the Spanish language, but also in a more extensive translation of the same work which he was to publish almost thirty years later.[13]

Free, then, of his bookkeeping duties and fully aware of some of the obstacles that loomed ahead, Puglia dedicated himself wholeheartedly to his literary task, and when he found that his writing was still not progressing as rapidly as he had hoped, he went so far as to dismiss most of his students of Spanish. (pp. vii-viii)

Although it is clear that Puglia recognized the financial problems that faced him, he was spurred on, it seems, by unquenchable optimism

---

Press, 1942); Harry Marlin Tinkcom, *The Republicans and Federalists in Pennsylvania, 1790-1801* (Harrisburg: Pennsylvania Historical and Museum Commission, 1950); Donald O. Stewart, *The Opposition Press of the Federalist Period* (Albany: State University of New York Press, 1969).

[13] See below, p. 59.

and a sense of mission. Nor were there lacking many good reasons for his buoyancy, the main one being a confluence of circumstances that seemed to make the moment propitious for the appearance of such a book as he had planned. In France the revolutionary government was firmly in the saddle and in many parts of the world the prestige of democratic ideas in general and of French enlightenment ideas in particular was high indeed, particularly in the United States where the newly formed government of the Convention, because it claimed to be operating under the banner of liberty and equality and was apparently emulating the revolutionary methods that the English colonies themselves had followed successfully a decade or so earlier, was looked upon with favor by many and perhaps most Americans. Exactly one week after Puglia gave up his bookkeeping job, on January 21, 1793, Louis XVI was guillotined by vote of the Convention and his execution, along with accounts of many horrifying atrocities, was destined to shake public opinion the world over and evoke dismay and doubts among many democrats. But several weeks would have to pass before this disquieting news could reach Philadelphia, and in the meantime Puglia was writing assiduously. Furthermore, he had friends, particularly the members of a Société des Amis de la Liberté, a group of French residents of Philadelphia who precisely in these days were organizing themselves into a society not unlike many another democratic club of the kind that existed in France, and in the United States as well, at this juncture in history. Fortunately, the minutes of the Societé's meetings have been preserved, and beginning with a session on February 3, 1793, this organization sought to become a force for disseminating French political ideas, cementing friendship between revolutionary France and the United States, and providing a bond among French democrats residing in the Philadelphia area. Active during the very tumultuous times of 1793, the Société fell victim to internal dissension and rapidly changing attitudes toward France and its revolutionary government, and the last meeting of the club recorded in its minutes was held in April, 1794.[14]

During Puglia's time of need in January, 1793, however, the Société was a new and vital force, and to some of its members Puglia undoubtedly refers in the passage already quoted above where he

---

[14] The minutes of the Société are in the library of the Historical Society of Pennsylvania in Philadelphia.

declares that some "Amigos de la Libertad" were urging him to finish his work. The fact is that at its meeting of February 24, 1793, the Société voted to subscribe to *one* copy of Puglia's forthcoming work, not a very generous aid to publication, to be sure, though it was undoubtedly assumed, at least by Puglia in his optimism, that some of the society's members would subscribe also as individuals.

Finally, on February 25, Puglia ingenuously laid his plans before the Philadelphia reading public by publishing *A Short Extract (Concerning the Rights of Man and Titles), from the Work entitled Man Undeceived, Written in Spanish by James Ph. de Puglia, Sworn Interpreter, Translated from the original by the Author, and corrected by a Democrat. In Confutation of Several Theological objections produced in an Aristocratical Piece by Walworth, against Thomas Paine, published in a London paper of the 7th of August, and in the Federal Gazette of the 13th of October last. Or rather Mr. Burke, under the name of Walworth. However, the Author confutes him as a different writer.* [15]

This small pamphlet in English is actually an appeal for subscriptions to the proposed longer work in Spanish. Puglia here translates for Philadelphia readers a portion of Chapter IV of *El desengaño del hombre*, which in the 1794 edition covers approximately pp. 87-100 of the completed work, a section that is a commentary on a few pages of Tom Paine's *Rights of Man*. Then the author declares:

> The above work is written in Spanish, that being the language the Author professes. The truth of the matter, the solidity of the arguments, together with the correctness of the style will enable the impartial citizens to form an adequate idea of its Author; who flatters himself, by such a proof, that hereafter he will have encouragement for other works which he has actually in hand.
> The Author conceives that the greater part of the Friends of Liberty in this country having no knowledge of the Spanish will become Subscribers merely to encourage the publication, without wishing to have all the copies they may subscribe for; he however leaves it to their usual generosity, requesting them in such case to express it.
> The generous light of Democracy which eminently shines forth in the American Stars, will in the publication of this

---

[15] (Philadelphia: Printed by Johnston & Justice, 1793). 16 pp.

work find a favourable opportunity of shewing how inclined it is to the propagation and support of the Rights of Man. [16]

Puglia's faith in Philadelphia's democrats was grievously misplaced. Having stated that he would wait a period of one month to gather sufficient subscribers, the would-be author found to his dismay that at the end of the appointed time he had obtained exactly *three* signatures! So disillusioned was he at this shattering display of Philadelphians' indifference that he promptly resolved to seek a more friendly climate for his democratic ideas by going to France, and he would have done so had he not been forced to desist because of his inability to scrape together enough money for his passage. (p. viii) Certain it is that the month of April was the low point in Puglia's budding career as a political writer, and his resignation on April 30 from his job as interpreter for the Commonwealth of Pennsylvania may have been an action, perhaps an overly hasty one, stemming from his sudden resolve to salve his disappointment in France. [17]

But if Puglia could not go to France, France would come to him, not as he had hoped when he waited in vain for a reply to his letter to the French Convention but in the person of Citizen Edmond Charles Genet, French Minister Plenipotentiary to the United States, who had arrived at Charleston, South Carolina, on April 8, 1793, and during Puglia's moments of deepest despondency was traveling northward in a leisurely manner toward Philadelphia to present to President Washington his credentials as the French Convention's first diplomatic representative in the U. S. capital.

Genet's brief and stormy career in the United States has been throughly studied on more than one occasion by both his defenders and his detractors. Whether the French Minister acted in accordance with the instructions he had received from his government, whether he conducted himself appropriately in attempting to gain the support of American public opinion, whether his acerbic protests to the U. S.

---

[16] Charles Evans in Vol. IX of his *American Bibliography* (Chicago: Columbia Press, 1925) states that the pamphlet (item. no. 26050) was distributed free on Philadelphia street corners, which is probably true. He is in error, however, when he says that Citizen Edmond Charles Genet paid for the publication of *this* work. See below, pp. 21 ff.

[17] Executive Minutes of Governor Thomas Mifflin (*Pennsylvania Archives*, 9th Series, I, 566).

government over the treatment of French privateers and their prizes in American ports were right and proper, and whether President Washington, Secretary of State Jefferson, and the cabinet were justified in demanding within three months of his arrival in Philadelphia that Genet be recalled to France are fascinating questions raised by his diplomatic mission, but they have no direct bearing on Puglia or *El desengaño del hombre,* so I shall not treat them here.

High on Genet's list of goals to be attained, however, was an ambitious but secret plan that looked toward nothing less than an attack by both diplomatic and military means upon the northern outposts of Spain's empire in America — Louisiana, Florida, and perhaps even Mexico — and one small facet of this larger effort is of vital concern to this study. I refer here not to Genet's hiring of secret agents who operated in Kentucky, New Orleans, and Florida nor to his attempts to organize in Kentucky a military invasion of the Mississippi valley under the command of General George Rogers Clark — this story has been told elsewhere [18] — but rather to what might be referred to, a bit facetiously perhaps, as Genet's surreptitious *literary* attack upon the northern flank of Spain's empire in the New World. I refer, of course, to *El desengaño del hombre.*

When Citizen Genet reached Philadelphia on May 16, he was, quite naturally, lionized by the various democratic groups that were flourishing in the city, [19] and among these the Société des Amis de la Liberté, as was predictable, played a particularly prominent role. Nor was anyone surprised when the Société elected the French Minister to membership in early June and to the presidency of the club on July 9. [20] Not recorded in any documents that I have been able to uncover is how or when Genet met Puglia, but clearly this was also to be expected in view of the latter's friendly ties with members of the Société, his enthusiasm for democratic principles, and particularly his admiration for France's revolutionary government. It is clear,

---

[18] See Link, pp. 134 ff.; also John Rydjord, *Foreign Interest in the Independence of New Spain; An Introduction to the War for Independence* (Durham, N. C.: Duke University Press, 1935), pp. 110-127.

[19] The German Republican Society of Philadelphia was organized in early April, and in May a Norfolk and Portsmouth Republican Society came into being in nearby Norfolk, Virginia. The Democratic Society of Pennsylvania adopted its constitution on June 3, 1793, shortly after Genet's arrival in Philadelphia. See Link, pp. 6-12.

[20] Minutes of June 1, June 8, and July 9.

moreover, that Puglia worked fast, seeing in Genet no doubt a providential source of the funds he so desperately needed to publish his book, and that he found Genet receptive to his urgent appeal. To the French diplomat Puglia's work *in Spanish* must have looked like a made-to-order psychological weapon that well might be wielded against public opinion in Spain's colonial possessions. The interests of the two men coincided, so on June 10 Genet lifted Puglia from his despondency by agreeing to finance his book.

Whether other persons were privy to the source of Puglia's sudden financial support can only be conjectured. When his book appeared, Puglia listed the names of twenty-three subscribers [21] who finally bought one to three copies of the work at one dollar each and included therein a discreet reference to an anonymous "Amigo verdadero de la libertad, e Independencia de todas las Naciones" who contributed no less than $130.00 toward publication costs of $153.00. After distributing twenty-nine books to subscribers and keeping one for himself, Puglia notes that four hundred and seventy of the edition of five hundred copies "Quedan a la disposición del democrático Mecenas." Not until 1821 did Puglia reveal in print that his mysterious benefactor had been Genet, [22] but there is no mistaking the sincere

---

[21] The short list of subscribers to the book reads like a who's-who of important political figures in Philadelphia and clearly indicates that Puglia had very good connections indeed. Besides Thomas Jefferson, Secretary of State, Alexander Hamilton, Secretary of the Treasury, and Governor Thomas Mifflin, the names of Benjamin Franklin Bache, grandson of Benjamin Franklin and an anti-Federalist newspaper publisher, Philip Freneau, widely acclaimed poet and politician, and John Swanwick, wealthy merchant and well known Francophile soon to be elected to the House of Representatives, attract particular attention. Of special interest to students of political and cultural relations between the United States and the Spanish world are the names of Joseph Ravara, Consul-General of Genoa in Philadelphia and also a subscriber to the *Mercurio Peruano* published in Lima at this same period in history, and Richard Meade, for about fifteen years after 1803 a merchant and U. S. diplomat in Spain. Some other names, though less important, belong to other people who were prominent in Philadelphia society.

[22] *El derecho del hombre, para el uso y provecho del género humano* (Filadelfia: Imprenta de H. Carey e Hijos, 1821), p. 168.

In the Genet Papers in the Library of Congress there is, among receipts for miscellaneous expenditures made in the latter part of 1793, an undated sheet of paper headed merely "2900. Doll." It lists, along with many other items adding up to a total of that amount, one payment of $130.00 to M. Bailey. This surely is the $130.00 that Puglia records as Genet's contribution toward the cost of publishing *El desengaño del hombre.*

gratitude that pervades the lines of the 1794 edition of *El desengaño del hombre* wherein Puglia thanked his anonymous financial angel.

The aspiring author's troubles, however, were not over. Plaintively he recounts his further vicissitudes:

> La órden por escrito fué dada en primer lugar a *Child y Swaine* Impresores de esta Ciudad. Tuviéron en su poder el Original desde mediado de junio hasta él de julio, en que no hallándose en estado de imprimirlo, substituyéron á *Francisco Bailey*, y de conformidad endosáronle dicha orden. (pp. viii-ix)

Then, after Bailey had dawdled a few weeks is getting the work out, no less a disaster than the devastating yellow fever epidemic of August, 1793, hit Philadelphia and Puglia's project. Practically the entire city and Bailey's printshop were abandoned, and to make matters worse, Bailey seemed to an anxious Puglia to have been an overly timorous soul:

> Si otros fuéron circumspectos en regresarse, Bailey mostró serle mas que todos, pues fué de los últimos que pareciéron en Ciudad. Volvió por último cerca el fin de Noviembre, y viendo que en lugar de apresurarse iba siguiendo con la misma pachorra, hízole el Autor sus quejas, á las quales respondió produciendo la falta de jornaleros, y las dificultades que naturalmente acarrea una impresion en un Idioma extrangero, y concluyó diciendo: que si el Autor se determinaba prestarle su asidua asistencia y auxilio, la publicación se aceleraría. (p. ix)

Although Puglia had recently found a new bookkeeping job, his dedication to the cause of liberty was equal to the challenge, so he once again gave up gainful employment in order to look after the pub-

---

A more formal financial accounting to the French government appears in some papers on secret expenses found in container 51 of the Genet Papers. In an official report headed *Compte des Dépenses secretes* there are *chapitres* dealing with the *Mission du Kentuckey*, the *Mission aux Illinois*, the *Mission à Boston, Propagande*, etc. In the section on *Propagande* three items are listed, two of which deal with payments to agents in New Orleans, Florida, and elsewhere. The third small item is entered as follows: "Payé à New York et Philadelphia pour publications, traductions & pamphlets propres â travailler l'Esprit public .....287." Almost certainly included in this expenditure of $287.00 is the $130.00 that went to Francis Bailey.

lication of his book, this time in the role of novice printer (i. e., "medioimpresor," as he humorously put it).

Having signed the last page of his manuscript on January 23, 1794, Puglia probably held in his hands the first copy of his printed work sometime during February, 1794. By this time it was obviously too late for the little book to be of any use to Genet personally, for he had been formally replaced as Minister by Citizen Joseph Fauchet in February, 1794, but this does not mean that the book's potential impact in the Spanish world was in any way lessened by Genet's dismissal. What became of the four hundred seventy copies of the book that were destined for Genet, I do not know; presumably they went to his successor, Citizen Fauchet, a much more cautious diplomat who came to his new post with an apparent determination to play things in a much lower key than his flamboyant predecessor. It is unlikely that Fauchet made any efforts to circulate them in the Spanish world. There is ample evidence, however, that at least two copies of Puglia's work penetrated the area where they were supposed to circulate and made a harsh impact upon Spanish officialdom. Before telling that story, however, it seems appropriate to examine the contents of *El desengaño del hombre* and see the reasons why this was so.

CHAPTER II

THE CONTENTS OF *EL DESENGAÑO DEL HOMBRE*

Although Puglia calls attention on the title page of his work to the fact that he is a "Maestro de la Lengua Castellana en esta metrópoli," his effort to put enlightenment ideas into Spanish for the edification of Spanish and Spanish American readers is seldom notable for the perfection of his language or the excellence of his literary style. Throughout his work it is evident that his is a strong personality — in modern parlance he would be called a "character" — and that the strength of his convictions and his capacity for vehement indignation frequently find forceful and sometimes quite effective expression in modes of style and thought that are notable for their vigor, though at times overly rhetorical in tone. Likewise of note, and nicely suited to the literary purpose that he set for himself, were Puglia's gift for caustic sarcasm, a taste for subtle and humorous irony (let his wry comment quoted above concerning Francis Bailey's slow return to Philadelphia stand as a small sample), and a penchant for stirring hortatory calls to political action. As passages from his work are cited below all of these qualities will, I think, be quite evident. Yet, although Puglia is usually effective and seldom dull, the organization of his material is not infrequently haphazard and his essays seldom display much literary polish. They will never be studied as models of their genre, nor will students of stylistic niceties or the skilful use of literary Spanish find much to hold their attention in the often incorrect and sometimes Italianate prose that Puglia writes. [1]

---

[1] Puglia himself seems to have been less than confident that his mastery of the Spanish language was equal to the demands being made upon it. At one point he addresses his reader:

Seekers after new or original ideas will likewise find little that is innovative in *El desengaño del hombre*. Although crammed with discussions of political questions and with disquisitions on many theoretical assumptions, the book, without ever mentioning Rousseau or any other of the French *philosophes* by name, clearly derives almost entirely from Rousseau's doctrine. Puglia is not an original thinker; his originality lies only in his gathering together many existing ideas and putting them into Spanish accompanied by numerous pointed comments and allusions which for the most part could refer only to the *Spanish* world. But even here Puglia, in an effort to pretend that his ideological attack is coldly objective and directed at despotism and the monarchical system wherever found, seeks as part of a studied pose to avoid, whenever possible, any direct reference to Spain or Spanish America by name. In fact he protests almost too loudly, though he may have been at least partially sincere in his protestations that his target is *all* despotic governments.² (p. 48) Like most eighteenth-century thinkers, Puglia instinctively seeks to deal in *universal* truths that are applicable to men everywhere, so he normally professes to be discoursing in general terms; and with the exception of some pointedly direct criticism of England and a few enthusiastic comments about France's new revolutionary government, he seldom refers to any specific country. But as he batters the monarchical system, rails against tyranny, censures courtly immorality, and hurls invective against scheming priests, the examples he cites, though usual-

---

El indulto que te pido no es tocante el sentido de mis periodos, sino en lo que respecta su explicacion y frases, las quales no son (lo confieso) de las mas correctas. Tal imperfeccion procederá á mi entender de la falta de cuidado en la ortografía, no porque dexe (como profesor) de saberla, sino que unos dicen que no entiendo el Español, otros que no soy capaz de escribir quatro comas, y así, lo mas acertado para mi es que me encomiende á tu fina comprehension é imparcialidad, de las quales espero merecer una cortez aceptación. (pp. 6-7)

Later in the book Puglia expressed somewhat similar sentiments. (p. 102)

² In one instance Puglia cites some abuses in Cuba and Mexico but advises his reader that "para no quebrantar la determinacion, que ha tomado [el autor] de no señalar por lo claro Reyno alguno ... procura disimular en quanto le es posible el nombre de los puertos en Cuba y Golfo de México." But then in his immediate use of the phrases "el Comercio de la H." and the "puerto de V. C." he can only be referring to Havana and Veracruz. (p. 60).

ly not identified as such, are, for the most part, Spanish examples, and the book as a whole stands as a passionate indictment of the entire Spanish system of government. When Spanish officialdom finally had a chance to examine the book, no officer of His Catholic Majesty entertained any doubts as to which king and which kingly system Puglia was seeking to destroy.

★ ★ ★

Puglia opens his book with a brief invocation "A la Santísima Magestad de Dios Todo Poderoso":

> Tu nombre invoco, SER SUPREMO, que por tu infinita bondad te dignas animar este miserable Escritor á la defensa de aquel Derecho, que desde el principio de los tiempos franqueaste á tu Humana Criatura. Plenamente conoces la integridad de esta Pluma, y con quanta razon hállase forzada á proclamar aquella verdad, que los zelos de los Soberanos obscurecen, ocultan y oprimen: dígnate pues como PADRE y PROTECTOR de la misma, promover su universal conocimiento á confusion de los TIRANOS, é IMPOSTORES.... Ilumina mi mente, inspira mi corazon y corrobora mi natural intrepidez, para que mis razonamientos no se desvíen de la pura verdad, y no me asuste el miedo de amenazas, pregones y asesinos. (pp. iii-iv)

Overblown though his rhetoric may be, Puglia obviously hoped that believers in God — and these would be the overwhelming majority of Spanish-speaking readers — would be moved by his pious appeal for divine approval of a work which, in calling upon God to instill valor in those who may *rise up* (i. e., *se levantaren*), hints at its revolutionary purpose even as it invokes the Deity.

The invocation is followed, as I have already stated above, by a page that lists the names of subscribers to Puglia's book, and this by a table of contents and a list of errata three pages long! The book proper begins with a *Prólogo* (pp. 1-7) which leads into four chapters of from twelve to thirty-two pages in length followed by a *Conclusión* (pp. 104-113). Finally, there is an important *Adición* (pp. i-xvii) which I have already mined extensively in tracing Puglia's life up to 1794.

Prólogo. The author opens his work by stating that certain authorities will disapprove of his book, but he professes unconcern as he declares solemnly that Reason will be his guide. He promises to write clearly and without sophistry, but he warns his reader that if he would understand his arguments, he must think without *passion*. His definition of passion, however, is indeed a strange one that seems peculiarly applicable to a country like Spain where, as many eighteenth-century thinkers had it, the weight of unenlightened traditionalism lay heavy upon the populace: "Entiendo por *pasion* aquella *credulidad,* que hémos adoptado á favor de nue[s]tros Antiguos, la qual nos avasalla á seguir sus pisadas, esto es, gemir baxo el peso de un usurpado Despotismo, sin que tampoco nos permita de considerar el desvalido derecho nuestro, ó (por lo claro) el *porque*." (p. 2) Yet, though he asserts that innumerable peoples endure this kind of slavery, Puglia claims that common men (i. e., *la plebe*) everywhere would be receptive to his ideas if their rulers would only permit them to hear the truth. But this, he asserts, will happen only with difficulty because sovereigns, the nobility, and the clergy "suelen amedrentar los ánimos de los Vasallos, y oponerse á que los pobres abran los ojos á la luz de la verdad, pues en teniéndolos vendados, consérvanse la quieta posesion de sus privilegios y Señorío." (pp. 2-3)

Then, addressing the reader in a personal way, Puglia entreats him as an individual to divest himself of his passion, since it makes a man "brutal, insensible y bueno para nada." Should he be so unfortunate as to be haunted by any kind of superstitious fear, Puglia warns, he should burn the book he is reading forthwith, but "si tu talento con el anhelo de apagar su sed en la fuente de la verdad es perseverante, sigue adelante y hallarás lo que buscas." (p. 3)

Adherence to reason is the key to success in this endeavor:

> Levántate pues de ese letargo amado lector quienquiera que seas; mira por ti, y considera que no hay mejor maestro para gobierno de tu vida y hechos que la Razon: á ella atente, con la misma aconséjate que nunca te será traydora. Recibióla el hombre de Dios no para sugetarla á otro ygual suyo, sino para que fuese su libre distintivo; la misma es la que te deve libertar de la dependencia que profesas, purificar de los perjuicios adoptados y constituirte en la pacifica posesion de lo que tontamente á otro tributas.... Si mis discursos te parecieren razonables, recibilos é imprimilos en tu corazon paraque te sirvan de guia en la execucion de la empresa, y si no llegaren á quadrarte haz lo que mejor te paresca y convenga, en la inteligencia que mas vale morir hon-

radamente en defensa de su derecho, que vivir con un vergonzoso disimulo baxo los pies de un detestable Usurpador. (pp. 5-6)

Puglia's call to Spanish readers to rebel against tyranny is thus clearly enunciated in his prologue even before he enters into the particulars of why despotism must be destroyed.

Chapter I, "El despotismo repugna á las leyes divinas y humanas." Puglia begins his attack with a truism. Noting ruefully that in monarchies the personal will or whims of kings are always supreme ("Allá van leyes donde quieren Reyes," as the proverb has it), Puglia mockingly asks:

> ¿Quien es este Campeon formidable, quien este Legislador? Es preciso sin duda que sea algun angel en distincion y entendimiento, ó que sepa á lo menos mucho mas de la humana sabiduria, para que sus decretos no admitan correccion: mas si este infalible nos parece y es (á pesar de nuestra alterada fantasía) un hombre como nos otros, quien gastó el tiempo de su educacion en las faldas de las Duquezas, y entre los alagos de las Cortesanas ¿que podrémos inferir? (p. 9)

His irreverent approach to royalty thus having been established, the author addresses himself to the origins of monarchy and kingly claims to represent God on earth. Noting that the Old Testament relates how the people begged Samuel to provide them a king in the person of Saul, Puglia opines that God, only with great reluctance and after repeated entreaties, finally yielded and permitted His people to have their king for the express purpose of proving to men the folly of their impertinent request. Citing the Bible for support of his interpretation, Puglia points out that men became aware of their loss of liberty only after it was too late for them to regain it from abusive sovereigns who claimed to have received their authority from God. (pp. 15-17)

In judging the claims of kings that their power derives from the Deity, Puglia counsels his readers to refer to their catechisms and to the Ten Commandments. Where, he asks, in His divine laws does God require that men obey kings? The fact is, of course, that the claims of monarchs are baseless and false: "Dios es buen padre, sabe lo que conviene, y hace lo que pide la felicidad de los hombres. No se declaró en favor de los Reyes, porque conoció no ser de justicia aprobar el paraiso de uno causando un infierno á millones." (p. 22) In considering the status of kings in human as opposed to divine law, Puglia, good disciple of Rousseau that he is, harks back to an earlier age of innocence before men fell under the tutelage of tyrants:

> Antes que hubiesen Reyes habian Leyes, y antes de pedir á Dios un Cabo... los pueblos se governaban de por si solos con ellas. Aquella primera edad de los hombres, que todavia no conocia ambicion, engaño ó violencia, es razonable de suponer que estableció leyes legitimadas sin afectacion con el sello de la Innocencia, y del Derecho Natural.... (p. 26)

Taking note of the outwardly joyful observances that customarily mark the crowning of a new king and seem to give evidence that monarchs enjoy popular acclaim, Puglia asserts that fear rather than love motivates such celebrations, (p. 27) and consideration of this problem leads him to devote considerable space to questioning the basic assumption that a dying king should have the right to bequeath his throne to his own son, who often turns out to be lamentably immature and inexperienced. How is it, asks Puglia, that the laws of Spain, Italy, and other nations permit a youth to come of age and manage his own affairs only at age twenty-five while callow young men of eighteen or twenty are routinely crowned as kings. The implications of this practice are obvious:

> El sentido de tales privilegios es tan necio, quanto es provocativo; intérnate en él y verás claramente que se dirige á sostener, de que para hacer uso de la Autoridad Real no se necesita sabiduria, y que se requiere solamente la Forma Material del hombre para ser Monarca. Si dixeran que para gastar el dinero del Público, vivir enteramente en el libertinage, y hacer lo que dicta el natural fanatismo es bastante un Bruto animal, entonces diré que los Reyes son muy aptos para eso, pues por lo que se ve no hacen otra cosa.... (p. 30)

Were a sovereign to send a mere boy to be a viceroy or governor, Puglia asserts, his vassals would refuse to receive such an official and with good reason: "Bastante motivo seria este para levantarse, y si así lo hicieran tendrian razon." (p. 33) Puglia does not at this point follow up the suggestion of possible rebellion contained in the line just quoted. Instead, he elaborates at some length on the problem of royal succession, young and inexperienced sovereigns, the need for talent and intelligence in rulers, and the folly of any free country that chooses to adopt a monarchical system of government. Furthermore, he categorically denies to any generation the right of surrendering to a king and his progeny the privilege of governing perpetually; and such abuses in the past now oblige the present generation to remove those kings whom its progenitors have foisted upon it:

> Supuesto que yo dixese, que los Muertos viven y los Vivos mueren... me responderias que soy falto de juicio, ó que no entiendes el enigma: voy á explicarme por lo claro. Los que nos vendieron (barato ó caro no lo sé) ó regalaron á los Señores Reyes viven en su voluntad, decretos y convenios mientras nos otros estamos agonizando baxo la opresion de los Tiranos; consiguientemente los que son en polvo viven, por la contra nos otros con carne y huesos estamos continuamente muriendo.... Tan injusta y nula fué la constitucion de las Monarquias, como es de legalidad, y rectitud el abolirlas del todo. (pp. 38-39)

Chapter II. "*Atrazos y daños, que el despotismo acarrea á la sociedad.*" Having destroyed some of the theoretical foundations of the monarchical system, Puglia now spotlights certain specific abuses and pinpoints their location. Three branches of government, or *secretarías,* he alleges, are the centers of despotic rule — *Estado, Hacienda,* and *Guerra* — and the prime requisites for serving in any one of them are that a prospective official be "*Noble, Rico y Pícaro.*" (p. 42)

Estado administers the Crown's business at home and abroad and it is "muy visible y notorio que los Embaxadores, Ministros, &c, no saben en que pasar el tiempo si no en combites, crápulas, teatros, tertulias, bayles &c, que les rinden perezosos, libertinos y pródigos." (p. 43) These aforementioned officials, and others too, seek only their personal gain and systematically neglect the interests of ordinary people. High posts and honors are almost always reserved for nobles, and "como que el Monarca es el Typo del orgullo, todos los adherentes á la Corona siguen en quanto les es permitido su exemplar." (p. 45) Haughty and vain in their dealings with those who are obliged to seek their favors, they extort money from the people in order to support their irregular personal habits ("... quien tiene un amorcito platónico, quien es amansevado y quien se huelga con las rameras..."

[p. 45]). So lucrative are some posts in officialdom that they are offered for sale — fifty thousand pesos for a viceroyship while archbishoprics go for from ten to thirty thousand — and money alone guarantees favors at court where concubines charge dearly for their recommendations to ministers.

No better is *Hacienda,* for "en lo perteneciente á despachos de qualquiera clase que sean, sigue exactamente la regla de la de Estado como hija que tambien ella es de la Gran Madre Monarquia." (p. 47) Puglia goes on to inventory the grafting, the dealing in contraband, and the other abuses in which the employees of this office engage. More than 86,000 employees work in *Hacienda,* and in a long footnote Puglia lists by categories the salaries received by each class of public servant. More than seventeen million *pesos fuertes* are needed to pay this horde, and the abuses and outright extortion, particularly the tax injustices, that the king's subjects suffer at the hands of these employees, are described in assiduous detail.

More essential to the preservation of despotism than either *Estado* or *Hacienda,* however, is the *Secretaría de Guerra*: "...sobre ella descansa el Cetro y la Corona, pues sin la fuerza el Despotismo caeria al suelo. Sobre esta basa elévase la ostentacion como pirámide, para que los Vasallos la tengan respecto, y los enemigos tiemblen á la vista de tan belicoso aparato." (p. 53) Again Puglia adds up rank by rank the excessive cost of maintaining some four thousand military and naval officers along with eighty regiments and eighty ships of war (p. 55), all this without counting the scandalous waste and graft which he himself had observed on a trip through the King's Arsenal a few months before his departure for America.

As in the case of the royal officials treated earlier, the gambling, whoring, and other immoralities of military officers cost huge sums which must come from the pockets of the king's subjects, and also as in the other royal services, poor men are systematically excluded from positions of rank and influence in favor of the nobility.

Worst of all, despotism requires occasional wars in order to perpetuate itself, and the indignant author describes the disastrous effect of such military ventures on the various classes of society and shows how, in the end, the burdens of all groups are shifted downward to the shoulders of the long-suffering common people. Not only are the poor compelled to labor in order to maintain their despot in power, but thousands of common soldiers are sent to their deaths in senseless

THE CONTENTS OF *EL DESENGAÑO DEL HOMBRE* 33

battles and for frivolous causes that are often against their own best interests. The present attacks upon the French Republic by Prussian armies prove the point. (pp. 62-63)

Chapter III, "*Sacudir el yugo del despotismo no ofende las máximas de religion.*" This is the shortest chapter in Puglia's book, but it is clear that the author himself considered it perhaps the most crucial of all in that it faces up squarely to what he conceived to be the greatest obstacle to acceptance of his ideas by Spanish readers: namely, the opposition of churchmen who use their influence to support despotism.

Puglia begins his discourse once again with a truism: "Escoger lo bueno á preferencia de lo malo es un instinto natural, que él que no lo sigue es stúpido y sin razon." (p. 66) With the example of France and the United States before them, he urges his readers to keep this in mind and to seek the truth.

At this point, however, the clergy enter the picture for they, Puglia charges, are bent on convincing the faithful that religion is closely tied to secular government. This premise he challenges with another: namely, that religion has nothing to do with secular government however much the clergy, which has a vested interest in perpetuating despotism, may seek to protect despots by teaching that an attack on the monarchical system is an assault on religious beliefs. (p. 67) Puglia's own credo holds that God is on the side of human liberty:

> Si la Religion fuese Dios (créeme hermano) no tendrian los Pueblos atajo alguno por este lado para lograr su libertad, pues á demas de ser neutral en una guerra tan justa, seria el Protector de las armas populares, porque su infinita rectitud no puede sino defender la razon y humiliar á los soberbios y tiranos: mas así no piensan los Ministros suyos, cuyo corazon en lugar de elevarse al Cielo busca rahices en la Tierra. (p. 68)

Friars and canons, Puglia charges, function as spies of the Inquisition, which was, in fact, expressly created in order to protect the throne. "Trátese ahora de sacudir el Yugo del Despotismo, y allá vá la Inquisicion contra el Pueblo como enemigo mortal; hé áqui la Religion mezclada con el seglar, lo espiritual con lo temporal, lo santo con lo profano, y de esta suerte todo se vuelve confusion, guerras y destrozos." (p. 69)

Worst of all, the faithful ingenuously allow themselves to be victimized by such tactics:

> Echan mano al Crucifixo, cárganse de cadenas en señal de penitencia, esclamaciones freqüentes, lágrimas á barato, allá va el pobre engañado pueblo contrito y lleno de santa intencion á los pies del predicador, sospirando y pidiendo á Dios perdon y misericordia por haber intentado el logro de su libertad, el recaudamiento de su hacienda, la conquista de su derecho natural. (p. 69)

Catholic clergymen oppose any kind of upheaval (i. e., *levantamiento*) on the grounds that if all men are placed on a level of equality the door will be opened to the entry into Catholic countries of all varieties of religions. To this objection Puglia replies simply that the presence of other sects "no puede causar daño alguno á la Católica dominante, antes bien añadirle gloria, y propagacion." (p. 72) Aware that the idea of tolerating heretics will shock his Spanish readers, Puglia seeks to convince them that the presence of non-Catholics is not undesirable in a Catholic country:

> No hay quien pueda negar de que en todas Religiones y Sectas hay buenos y malos, letrados é ignorantes, afables y soberbios, consiguientemente hallaránse en cadauna de ellas hombres honrados, hábiles y dignos de ocupar un asiento en el Congreso, ó Consejo de Estado....
>
> El absurdo mas grande que un Pueblo pueda adoptar, y que (á pesar de la razon) echó rahices entre los Italianos y Españoles es, de pensar que un Protestante no hace cosas á derechas por ser de diferente religion, y (segun dicen ellos) *condenado* como si la honradez, sabiduria y crianza no se pudiesen hallar en otra parte, que entre los Católicos. Uno de estos soy yo y por tal me declaro, pero no peco de semejante temeridad, pues llegó la experiencia á convencerme de lo contrario, y con tanta evidencia que estoy para afirmar (a mi propia confusion) que hay mayor exemplaridad, industria y buena fé entre los Protestantes, que los Católicos. (pp. 72-73)

Though insistent that tolerance must be part and parcel of real religion, Puglia ends his discussion on an orthodox and reassuring note calculated to strike a responsive chord in his Catholic readers: "La Verdad es una sola, y la Palabra de Dios es inalterable; conque siendo la Católica el único medio para lograr la vida eterna, ha de resplandecer como diamante entre cristales." (pp. 75-76)

Chapter IV, "La libertad é ygualdad del govierno forma la felicidad de la nacion." If in the preceding chapters Puglia has told his readers what is wrong with monarchy, he seeks now, partly by theorizing and partly by citing concrete examples, to convince them of the advantages of democracy. Working from an initial premise that "no hay ni puede haber paz sin libertad, ni libertad sin paz," (p. 78) Puglia summarizes some contemporary ideas about the physical universe (its elements, bodies at rest, its perfect order, the freedom of plants and other unfeeling bodies, etc.) in order to prove not only that God himself is free but that "es pues absolutamente indispensable que todo lo que la misma [i. e., la omnipotencia de Dios] crea sea libre." (p. 79) Included, of course, is man, though history shows that he often fails to protect the God-given freedom that he possesses. Theorizing further, Puglia discourses on society and its relationship to government ("La Sociedad forma el Gobierno y no el Gobierno la Sociedad...."), and he holds that "siendo pues incontrastable que toda Nacion es libre quiera ó no quiera, sale la conseqüencia que el Gobierno establecido directamente por ella, es libre tambien." (p. 80) Seeking to refute those who assert that the inevitable effect of laws must be to take away freedom, Puglia essays to show through fairly standard arguments that the functioning of laws actually increases it. Although he writes here mostly in a theoretical vein, Puglia lets pass no opportunity to hurl barbs in the direction of despotic governments in general and the British government in particular. However, he returns quickly to his main thesis: "El requisito esencial é inseparable de una verdadera libertad, es la perfecta Ygualdad." (p. 83) The latter is "una ley inalterable de naturaleza" and "un equilibrio general y necesario á la quietud," (p. 84) and this happy state of affairs is to be found only under a democratic system that treats all men alike. (p. 84)

To confound those skeptics who hold that in the absence of social distinctions there can be only chaos, Puglia invites doubters to spend some time in a democratic republic and observe for themselves not only the degree to which governors and governed respect each other's freedom and equality while living in harmony, but also the process whereby men rise to positions of authority solely on the basis of ability, not social position. Only democracy with its understanding of equality knows what real subordination is as distinguished from the blind and servile humility and subjection that monarchies demand. From democracy's healthy insights into this problem it develops much of its strength, as has been recently proved by the military successes of the United States. (p. 86)

At this point Puglia digresses a bit. The subject he is discussing calls to mind recent polemics between Tom Paine and Edmund Burke, and Puglia is moved to essay a defense of Paine. The latter's *Rights of Man*, written to refute a work by Burke that had been critical of the French Revolution, had in its turn evoked a rejoinder from Burke writing under the pseudonym of Walworth. Equality was the subject under discussion and Walworth, affecting the role of a learned theologian, had marshalled theological arguments from as far back as the time of Adam and Eve in support of nobility and social inequality. Puglia, of course, flails away at Walworth's undemocratic ideas with all the weapons in his arsenal. The dozen pages or so that he devotes to his attack on Walworth are most interesting and they are important in that they contain, as far as I know, the first discussion of Tom Paine's works to appear anywhere in Spanish, but they are basically restatements of Puglia's abiding belief in freedom and equality for all men (and women too)[3] and reiteration of his criticism of the nobility and all forms of privilege before the law. Hence, rather than dwell here on these repetitions, important though they undoubtedly were to the author himself, I shall direct attention toward only two passages whose facetious tone, unlike the deadly serious paragraphs that are Puglia's normal stock in trade, gives a new and unexpected dimension to Puglia's mode of writing. Having noted that Walworth defends social inequities by arguing that God made Eve inferior to Adam, Puglia indulges in some sly humor, though it is marred by some heavy-handed and needless moralizing at the end:

> Me alegraria de saber si Walworth es casado ó cortejó en su tiempo alguna muchacha, como tambien si entre los requiebros de la conversacion la mentó semejante proposi-

---

[3] On pp. 87-89 Puglia shows himself to be an early defender of women's rights. For his comments on his own marital status, see below pp. 52.

cion, pues tengo para mí que eso solo hubiera bastado para hacerse despreciar, no digo de una doncella bonita, pero de una vieja fea y asquerosa. Yo por mi parte pisé (como es notorio) hasta por la presente la verea de los solteros, y aunque sea del todo ignorante en lo de cortejar, paréceme las trataria con mayor comedimiento de este filósofo grosero. ¡Infeliz el hombre que aborrece la muger, única joya de valor que él pueda hallar en este valle de amargura para suavizar los ratos de su vida transitoria! (p. 89)

By way of ridiculing the noble class a few pages later, Puglia again has recourse to humor, this time of the unsubtle variety:

Uno de los Misterios aristocráticos es de suponer y creer firmemente, que quando el Rey se digna crear Noble algun Plebeyo, vuelve pura y quilatada aquella sangre que un minuto antes era baxa, vil y vulgar; siendo pues tan mirable la virtud del real cumplimiento, preciso es que reconoscamos á todos los Reyes por Santos en vida, siendo así que cada creacion de Noble es un Milagro. Quiero desde luego figurar que el tal hombre antes de volverse *caballero* sea tuerto ó cojo, y parece natural que mientras S. M. se sirve purificar la masa interior de la sangre, pueda de la misma suerte perfeccionar la fealdad exterior del sujeto privilegiado. A este tenor la Señoria de las Cortes deviera ser el emporio de la hermosura, y el echizo de las gentes, pero demasiado notorio y visible es á todo individuo que ve una Corte, de que hay Duque y Señor, cuya cara es mas fea y asquerosa que la de un cochino; y si formamos una idea del alma en proporcion del cuerpo, la cuenta que saco por regla de trés, me lleva la noticia segura que en las personas de muchos Príncipes, Marqueses, Condes &c. &c. caben solamente almas de borricos transmigrados. (pp. 93-94)

Such moments of levity, even sarcastic levity, are, however, rare in *El desengaño del hombre*, and most of what Puglia writes is unremittingly serious in its intent. So he loses little time in getting back to the theme of liberty and equality, and he ends his chapter with a utopian picture of democratic government as he conceives it, basing his description presumably on life as he has observed it in the United States. The individuals who make up the Congress, he would have his reader believe, always speak and act in the name of their constituents, and their deliberations are in the open and freely discussed because all persons have the inviolable right to speak or to publish their opinions without hindrance. Information about the expenditure of public funds flows freely through the newspapers, and wise economic policies encourage commerce, manufacturing, and the arts to the increasing prosperity and happiness of all. Foreigners, attracted by the hospitality and good faith of the democratic government, come to live under its benign protection and become good citizens. Religious differences cause no problems because each individual follows the dictates of his own conscience. Finally, democracy seldom goes to war except under provocation, but if conflict becomes inevitable, it is capable of waging war effectively because the reasons for fighting are openly discussed. (p. 102)

Conclusion. Puglia's final chapter opens with a modest disclaimer by the author. After begging his reader's pardon for not having done as much perhaps with his subject as his title promised, he seeks to disarm any critics by stating publicly that "no tengo reparo de confesarlas [i. e., las faltas de mi talento] buenamente, para que el Sabio que me tachare de ignorante, sepa que nada de nuevo dice con eso." (p. 104)

Before settling down to the serious business of framing the exhortation to his readers that is to make up the body of his conclusion, Puglia also takes note of the fact that his discussion of monarchical and democratic governments has omitted any real consideration of government *by* the aristocracy as such. This oversight Puglia proceeds to correct, at least partially, in a few paragraphs dedicated to the proposition that "no hay peor Gobierno en el Mundo que la Aristocracia. Baxo la capa de República encubre la tirania mas austera. Es una especie de Despotismo esparcido entre los Nobles...." (p. 105)

Having thus warned any uncautious person against contemplating government by the aristocracy as a possible alternative to monarchical despotism, Puglia closes his book by exhorting his oppressed readers to seek in democracy a solution for their political woes:

> ¡Pueblos amados, que todavia no teneis la nocion agradable de una completa libertad! Dios permita que la tengais con aquella énfasis y resolucion, que muestra al dia de hoy la pulida Nacion Francesa.... Consuelo y proteccion aguarden aquellos, que quisieren emprender la misma verea, que ella pisó para llegar al descansado Parnaso de la Libertad.... (p. 105)

Warning any would-be democrat to guard against the many secret spies of despotism, Puglia professes confidence that a Messiah will soon appear to lead the way to democracy. Then in tones much more cautionary than some of the optimistic prognoses which he had sometimes indulged in earlier, the author warns that much will depend upon the character of the new leader and upon the ability of the politically oppressed to recognize him:

> Parecerá el Mesia os lo predigo, pero Dios quiera que os sea fiel, y saque felizmente del laberinto. Si su apariencia es tal, obedecedlo y respetadlo, que bien lo merece por el riezgo á que se expone, pero antes de todo mirad que no sea falto de los tres requisitos, que voy á decir para vuestra instruccion. SABIO, esto es, que haya dado adelantadas pruebas de un talento esclarecido, y que tengais confianza en el plan, que su prudencia y habilidad os proponga. POPULAR, siendo enemigo de honras, afable y amigo. VALIENTE, para que los peligros, amenazas y muerte no le asusten hasta el último momento de su vida. Si tal hombre teneis, no os dé cuidado alguno que vais seguros, y mucho no tardaréis á ver en pedazos aquellos grillos y cadenas, que cruelmente os tienen amarrados en el calabozo de vuestra infelicidad.[4] (p. 106)

Such is Puglia's call to rebellion, and in the several pages which follow he does not stint on the advice which he gives to prospective revolutionists about how they should conduct themselves as they seek to shape new forms of government. But he displays some hard-headed realism as he cautions against needless bloodshed and cruelty, particularly cruel vengeance against the enemies of democracy, and exhorts his readers to be alert to the dangers of civil strife. Vitally important also is great care in the election of honorable men as the people's representatives.

"Venerad al Clero," Puglia counsels his readers, "si su conducta es en perfecta neutralidad, pero no os aconsejeis con él en puntos políticos de Estado.... [y] clamad al instante contra el Frayle im-

---

[4] In 1822 Puglia was to lay claim to having prophesied here the rise of Simón Bolívar:

> I appeal, without vanity, to the *conclusion* of the above work [i. e., *El desengaño del hombre*], to evince the most *clear literal* prophecy of what has lately taken place in South America. I positively asserted, that a political redeemer would appear among them, who, possessing the requisites therein described, would soon break their chains and make them free. By comparing said contents with the heroic deeds of that immortal founder of Spanish American Liberty, SIMON BOLIVAR ¿who can hesitate in pointing him out, though a *minor* at the time, as the saviour of his country then announced by me? (*Forgery Defeated*, p. 22)

prudente, que con un crucifixo en la mano se esfuerza persuadiros lo que es contra vuestro interés, bien y felicidad, porque en aquel momento no es palabra de Dios la que escuchais, sino una maligna amplificacion de un falso Ministro." (pp. 108-109) "Estad bien con Dios," advises Puglia in his last words on the subject, "el qual sin los sermones de los Frayles os hablará al corazon, y os dictará el método con que deveis seguir para descansar luego en una quieta libertad." (pp. 110-111)

His essential message delivered, Puglia in the last three pages of his work sets down in capsule form a few basic eighteenth-century articles of faith that underlie all that he has written:

> Nace el Hombre en el Mundo, y como miembro de la Sociedad aguarda esta de él aquellas ventajas, que su talento promete; es desde luego una obligación indispensable de este individuo de aplicarse á favor de la misma en todo lo que él se crée hábil, para mejorar las faltas de los que carecen de ygual entendimiento. El título de *paisano, amigo, hermano,* es un gran estímulo para un alma bien inclinada y sensible. Tal es la lealtad, industria y constancia de la misma que no vive para sí, sino para sus cohabitadores: y ninguna dificultad tuviera de sacrificar su vida para promover la felicidad de sus vecinos. Esto se llama cumplir plenamente al dever, que con nosotros nació, esto es ser un árbol fecundo en el jardin de la Sociedad, y por este medio llega la humana Creatura á merecer por todo derecho el título de HOMBRE. (pp. 111-112)

Finally, in lines which exude lofty if somewhat naive optimism, Puglia concludes:

> Este es el Siglo de la universal reforma, mediante la qual los Pueblos llegarán otra vez á verse HOMBRES....
>
> Despliéguese pues en nombre de Dios el glorioso Pavellon de la Libertad, para que aliviadas las Gentes de la despótica Opresion, sean mas intencionadas á servirle, amarle y adorarle. Baxo tan delicioso auspicio recójanse á descansar los pobres fatigados de la Tirania, y la trompa de la terrena Redencion lleve la noticia de la dichosa Libertad americana y francesa, para que toda la redondez de la Tierra imite su exemplar; y por último como que no hay, ni puede haber otra legítima Soberanía que la del Pueblo, diga este con alborozo, determinación y constancia: MUERA EL REY, VIVA LA LEY. (p. 113)

CHAPTER III

EL DESENGAÑO DEL HOMBRE IN THE SPANISH WORLD

In late October, 1794, worshippers in Mexico City found posted in their churches a large broadside which bore at the top in bold black letters the heading "NOS LOS INQUISIDORES APOSTOLICOS" and went on to greet its readers in the name of Jesus Christ. Then came these ominous words:

> SABED: QUE CON ASOMBRO, Y GRAVE dolor de nuestro corazon, hemos leído y exâminado, y hecho exâminar â nuestros zelosos, y sabios Calificadores un Libro en octavo intitulado: Desengaño del Hombre, impreso en Filadelfia en este presente año, su Autor D. Santiago Felipe Puglia. Este infame Autor se manifiesta por su Obra, orgulloso, altivo, inobediente, blasfemo, traidor, y con todos los demás caractéres conque describe San Pablo en la segunda Carta á Timoteo, capítulo tercero, aquella casta de hombres que aparecerán en los últimos dias, que segun parece se acercan, é instan ya....

Taking note of the blasphemies against God, the Catholic religion, and the King that Puglia's book contains, the edict proceeds to condemn the author who "desde un rincón del Orbe, toca su ronca trompeta, para excitar â la revelion mas infame, â la mas enorme traycion, y â una horrenda Anarquia â los fieles pueblos de la Nacion española, escribiéndoles en su idioma, que él mismo ignora." Though the Inquisitors state that as yet they have received no word that the execrable volume has actually circulated in their district, the present proclamation pointedly reminds the populace that several earlier edicts, most notably one dated March 13, 1790, have already prohibited the possession of any papers, tracts, or books whatsoever about the French

Revolution, and then condemns this particular book in vigorous language ("... le prohibimos in totum, aun para los que tienen licencia de leer Libros prohibidos..."). Finally, it demands under penalty of excommunication and fine that all citizens surrender within six days any copies of the book that they may own, and also that they denounce any third person known to be in possession of the condemned work.[1]

That Puglia had hit the mark with his book is obvious — at least he had given the Mexican inquisitors a bad case of the jitters — but whether they actually had much reason to be alarmed is another question.

★ ★ ★

The fascinating story of Spanish officialdom's reaction to *El desengaño del hombre* begins when a French corsair put into the port of Philadelphia with a prize, a Spanish brigantine, the San José de las Animas, commanded by Captain Juan Díaz de Castro. Released by the government of the United States, Díaz sailed south to Florida where on July 17, 1794, he reported in Saint Augustine to Governor Juan Nepomuceno Quesada with his ship, his men, and at least two copies of Puglia's book. One of these Díaz, apparently acting on his own initiative, sent directly to Don Luis de las Casas, Captain General of Cuba and Florida in Havana, and the other he showed to Quesada. The Governor's quick perusal of the book led him to write a hasty letter dated July 19 to the Conde de Revillagigedo, Viceroy of New Spain. Quesada informs the Viceroy that under questioning the Spanish captain had told him that "en Filadelfia se había establecido una nueva imprenta, en que se estampaba cierta obra muy perjudicial a la quietud de la Monarquía, de la que traía consigo un ejemplar que me entregó con el buen fin de que el govierno adoptase las medidas que hallase por convenientes para evitar su introducción, a cuyo fin me dijo había remitido otro a la Capitanía General de la Isla de Cuba y estas Floridas." Quesada's own alarm is clearly stated:

> En efecto, examiné el librito y lo hallé concebido bajo unas máximas muy perniciosas, y a mi corto entender, dirigidas expresamente a la España, pues a más de estar en su

---

[1] Archivo General de Indias (Sevilla), Legajo 3 (Estado México).

idioma, citando casos de nuestro Gobierno y Puertos de nuestra América, entra con la capa de religión, para ser leído y admitido con más gusto, de modo que comprendo pueda ser muy perjudicial entre el pueblo ignorante, animado por malignos espíritus que nunca faltan. [2]

This letter to Revillagigedo and the copy of the pernicious volume were channeled, of course, through the office of Las Casas in Havana, and the latter, on September 12, 1794, sent these items on to Mexico with a covering letter addressed to the Marqués de Branciforte, who had replaced Revillagigedo as Viceroy on July 12, 1794. Surprisingly, Las Casas professes not to have received the first copy of Puglia's book that Díaz sent him, but he writes the Viceroy that to him he is remitting without delay the second one obtained from Quesada. [3]

Upon receipt of the volume and Las Casas' communication, Branciforte, new to his post and already engaged in a vigorous campaign against French sympathizers in Mexico and all books about the French Revolution, [4] moved quickly to meet the threat posed by the new danger. In a letter to Don Manuel Godoy, Duque de Alcudia and

---

[2] *Los precursores ideológicos de la guerra de independencia, 1789-1794,* Vol. I (México: Talleres Gráficos de la Nación, 1929), pp. 235-236.

[3] Ibid., p. 235. Quesada in his letter of July 19 cited above seems to have feared that Las Casas would not receive the book Díaz sent. He tells Revillagigedo that he is sending the second copy of *El desengaño del hombre* through Las Casas "... para que, si la casualidad hiciese no haber recibido el volumen que Díaz le remitió, no carezca S. E. de tan importante noticia." One wonders what became of the first copy. Interesting too is the haste with which Las Casas got rid of the book. In the letter written to Branciforte on September 12, he says that he must send the work along without having read it "... como en este momento acabo de recibirlo y la salida del correo se ha señalado para el día de mañana...." Fourteen days later when he reports to the Minister of War in Madrid, he explains that he could not read it "... como llegáse la tarde misma en que debian embarcarse los pliegos p.ª Veracruz..." (Archivo General de Indias, Papeles de Cuba, Legajo 1484, Carpeta D, Carta No. 443), and in a letter to the Governor of Louisiana dated the same day he again explains that he did not ascertain what was in it "por la contingencia de embarcarse los pliegos para Veracruz la tarde misma que la recibí...." (Archivo General de Indias, Papeles de Cuba, Legajo 152B, Carpeta Septiembre, Carta No. 202).

[4] Although Revillagigedo had for some time been issuing orders against the spread of seditious ideas, rumor had it that the Viceroy, himself American born and considered by some to be tainted with French ideas, had not moved with as much vigor as the situation demanded. Branciforte acted energetically to correct this omission. See *Los precursores,* introduction by Nicolás Rangel, pp. LV ff.

Prime Minister in Madrid, Branciforte, after reporting on some of the very efficacious measures he has been taking against certain Frenchmen, wrote the following on October 3, 1794:

> Tranquilo en esta parte, no puedo estarlo con los avisos que acabo de recibir del Gobernador de la Habana, constantes en los documentos que comprende la carpeta número 4, pues los colonos americanos, aspiran a la libre navegación del río Misisipi, reúnen fuerzas para conseguir sus designios y permiten en Filadelfia la libre impresión de un nuevo libro, hasta el extremo abominable, con el título de *Desengaño del Hombre*, intentando introducirlo en este Reino por el Nuevo Orleans. [5]

He outlines reasons why a dangerous situation exists, particularly in New Orleans, because of the presence of too many unassimilated French inhabitants, and then lists counter measures which he has devised there and on New Spain's northern borders, among them the following: "Trasladaré las [novedades] del día al Comandante General Independiente de las Provincias Internas, don Pedro de Nava, a fin de que, como responsable de ellas, sirvan de gobierno a sus disposiciones y dicte las que juzgue más convenientes para impedir la introducción del referido libro sedicioso." [6]

Before implementing this plan, however, the Marqués de Branciforte waited for the Inquisition to pass judgment on Puglia's work, and after the condemnation which I have discussed above was forthcoming on October 24, the Viceroy five days later sent a copy of the edict to Nava along with instructions to keep the book from coming into New Spain through Texas and Coahuila, the areas under his personal jurisdiction. At the same time he assures Nava that he himself has initiated "las providencias más eficaces" to prevent its entry through the port of Veracruz and the colony of Nuevo Santander. [7]

---

[5] *Los precursores*, p. 160. Rydjord notes reports that three hundred copies were to be sent into the country by way of New Orleans (*Foreign Interest*, pp. 128-129). He cites this letter of October 3, 1794, from Branciforte to Alcudia as his source, but as printed in *Los precursores* it contains no mention of the three hundred copies. The figure does appear, however, in various orders of the Inquisitors of New Spain dated between October 19, 1794, and January 8, 1795 (Vol. 1248, Papeles de la Inquisición — México, Fols. 196-209, in the Archivo General de la Nación in Mexico City).

[6] *Los precursores*, p. 161.

[7] Archivo General de Indias, Legajo 3 (Estado México).

EL DESENGAÑO DEL HOMBRE IN THE SPANISH WORLD 45

Since Las Casas had already written from Cuba to the Baron de Carondelet, Governor of Louisiana, on September 26 warning him that he should take "las providencias que considere conducentes áfin de interceptar su curso, y evitar por unos medios prudentes el incremento que podría acarrear un libelo dirigido á conmover el [sic] opinion de las gentes," [8] Viceroy Branciforte could at this point feel confident that all points of potential danger had been covered. What he could not know was that Genet's plan to send George Rogers Clark's army down the Mississippi had foundered the previous winter along with his own diplomatic fortunes and that his successor Fauchet was, as far as is known now, making no effort to circulate Puglia's book in New Spain or anywhere else. Had he been aware of these things he undoubtedly would have slept better during the latter months of 1794.

Soon to add to the alarm, however, was news that some ominously similar developments were taking place farther south in Spain's American possessions and that the Viceroy of New Granada, Don José de Ezpeleta, was, like Branciforte, experiencing some very anxious moments. Much better known to historians than the Puglia episode is the publication in Santa Fe de Bogotá of a Spanish translation of the French *Droits de l'homme* in late December or the first days of 1794 by another propagandist, Antonio Nariño, and it is to this event that I refer now. So alarmed was Ezpeleta at the appearance of Nariño's dangerous publication that on September 9 he sent a warning to Don Luis de las Casas in Havana to be on the lookout for it, and he described its content and general appearance in considerable detail so that the Captain General would recognize it if the work turned up in his territory. [9] Las Casas, with *El desengaño del hombre* fresh in his mind but lacking any personal knowledge of the work — it will be recalled that he claimed he did not read it when it passed through his hands — immediately leapt to the conclusion that the two subversive publications, the one out of Philadelphia and the other from Bogotá, were in all likelihood the same work in different formats and indeed that they probably represented two prongs of a well coordi-

---

[8] Archivo General de Indias, Papeles de Cuba, Legajo 152B, Carpeta Septiembre, Carta No. 202.

[9] Documento 79, Copia, Reservado, Oficio del Virrey de Sta Fé al Cap^{an} gral de la Isla de Cuba. In José Manuel Pérez Sarmiento, ed., *Causas célebres a los precursores* (Bogotá: Imprenta Nacional, 1939), I, 238.

nated conspiracy against the Spanish crown. In his reply to Ezpeleta, Las Casas therefore recounts how he came to see a copy of *El desengaño del hombre* and informs the Viceroy of his reaction to the warning just received:

> Aunque la brevedad con que salia el Buque para Veracruz, en que remití al Sor. Virrey el citado Pliego, no me dio tiempo de leer despacio el Impreso, concivo, segun las especies que conservo, ser el mismo de que me trata V. E., pero de distinta figura o enquadernacion, siendo creible que su Autor habrá ideado este diferente disfraz para mejor difundirlo y propagarlo en los Dominios Españoles de America; y sin embargo de que esto me daba motivo de aumentar mi vigilancia para precaver la introduccion de semejantes Papeles revolucionarios, ya tenia anticipadas mis medidas al efecto, de modo que haviendoseme avisado que un Buque Parlamentario de la Nueva Orleans, que llegó aqui á su regreso de Philadelphia, podia traher algunos de los Papeles de esta clase acordé con el Administrador de Rentas Reales se conociesen hasta los Equipages de la Tripulacion á pretexto de descubrir generos de Contrabando, bien que resultó no ser cierto este aviso pues no se encontró papel alguno sospechoso.[10]

So wrote Las Casas from Havana on October 17, 1794.

All these things having transpired in America, Viceroy Branciforte on November 3 again reported to the Duque de Alcudia in Madrid on developments since his last letter about *El desengaño del hombre*, written on October 3. With this new communication he sent not only the book itself but also a copy of its condemnation by the Inquisition in New Spain. He also included a copy of his instructions of October 29 to Pedro de Nava.

The consequence of all this was speedy action in Spain on the part of Alcudia and the Cardinal Archbishop of Toledo, the Inquisitor-General. On December 15, Alcudia requested the Inquisitor to give the book his attention. On February 9, 1795, the latter reported to Alcudia that the Council of the Inquisition had prohibited *El desengaño del hombre* in all the dominions of His Catholic Majesty,[11]

---

[10] Ibid., p. 239.

[11] Archivo General de Indias, Legajo 3 (Estado México). The text of the Inquisitor's letter indicates that he is replying to Alcudia's communication of December 15.

and on February 19, the Duque de Alcudia acknowledged receipt of the Cardinal-Archbishop's letter.[12] So ended the flurry of excitement caused by the entry of *El desengaño del hombre* into the Hispanic world. Spanish officialdom's frantic concern was actually much ado about very little since, at least until now, I have been able to discover no evidence whatsoever that any copies of the 1794 edition of Puglia's work, except for the two that Captain Díaz brought down from Philadelphia, ever made their way into the hands of Spanish American readers.[13] It is not impossible, of course, that some did and that they may turn up in public or private libraries in Spanish America, but if so, they apparently achieved their subversive mission silently and did not attract the attention of Spanish officials.

On the Philadelphia-Madrid axis, however, the story is not quite complete. Following instructions from His Catholic Majesty, the Spanish ministers in Philadelphia, Don José de Jaudenes and Don José Ignacio de Viar, in July, 1795, protested formally to Secretary of State Edmund Randolph about the publication on U. S. soil of Puglia's anti-Spanish book, and they demanded that its author and the printer of the volume be duly punished.[14] Randolph replied with a curt note stating that President Washington could not honor such a protest because he and his government were powerless to interfere with freedom of the press in the United States. He also pointedly reminded the Spanish diplomats that two years earlier, when they had made a similar protest about some criticism of Spain that had appeared in a Philadelphia newspaper, Thomas Jefferson, then Secretary of State,

---

[12] Ibid.

[13] The reappearance of *Desengaño del hombre* on a list of prohibited books issued by the Mexican Inquisition on a broadside dated July 8, 1797, may suggest that the Inquisition had reason to believe that the book was still circulating in New Spain three years after it was initially banned. The broadside is in the Lilly Library of Indiana University.

[14] Exactly what kind of measures should be taken against the author and printer are not specified in the text of the complaint, which reads: "En esta atencion paso à representar a nombre del Rey contra el Autor y contra el Ympresor esperando que las providencias que el Poder Executivo tomase seran satisfactorias a S. M. y capaces de desvanecer el concepto tan indiferente que debe haber formado de las seguridades de sincera amistad que el Rey se ha lisonjeado hasta ahora le profesaban los Estados Unidos." (Archivo Histórico Nacional, Estado, Legajo 3896, Apartado 1, Carta No. 303) Certainly this text, strong though it is, does not justify Puglia's claim that the Spanish government demanded that the United States deliver his person to the Spanish authorities. See p. 66. below.

had rejected their complaints on the same grounds, and in order to refresh their memory Randolph included with his own reply a copy of Jefferson's earlier letter.[15] Don José Ruiz de Santayana, the Spanish official who was handling matters in the absence of Jaudenes and Viar from Philadelphia, dutifully sent all of this correspondence to Alcudia with an acrid covering letter that in a few short lines summed up his frustration and disgust with the way freedom of the press and popular government operated in Philadelphia: "... podrá inferir S. M. que en un Pais de libertinage, como este, y en el que las Leyes estan de parte del Pueblo, no hay otro recurso que hacerse sordos a las desverguenzas de los Insolentes."[16]

---

[15] The text of Randolph's note and the copy of Jefferson's earlier letter are in the Legajo 3896 cited above.
[16] Ibid.

CHAPTER IV

MORE ON PUGLIA'S BIOGRAPHY, 1794-1822

If Puglia's moment of dubious glory at the court of Spain and in the offices of the Inquisition had passed, his life and his writing career had hardly reached their mid-point in 1795. Yet, except for a few Philadelphians who read Spanish, Puglia was in 1795 still completely unknown as an author save for the sixteen-page throw-away pamphlet in English that he had published in 1793 with a vain hope of finding subscribers for *El desengaño del hombre*. This situation was not to last very long, for in 1795 he published his most scholarly work, a long and, on the whole, very decorous book in English, *The Federal Politician*, wherein he sought to study in a deliberately calm and measured manner the workings of the democratic system and also to voice his own faith in popular government as he saw it evolving in the United States and France. Although Puglia is ever the thorough democrat whose unwavering conviction that mankind could be governed through popular processes is equal to every test, the contrast, which he himself points out, between this carefully reasoned analysis of democracy and his earlier emotional diatribes against despotism cannot fail to surprise readers familiar with *El desengaño del hombre*. In *The Federal Politician* Puglia consciously assumed the stance of an idealistic but coolly rational student of politics, and he generally succeeds in playing this carefully cultivated role from the first to the last page of his book.

August of 1796 found Puglia still writing in English, but the quiet analyst of political institutions and practices who produced *The Federal Politician* has departed the scene. William Cobbett, an English immigrant to the United States and former member of democratic groups, has renounced his earlier associations and now from his stationer's store with blue windows situated opposite Christ Church in Philadelphia has been issuing antidemocratic political pamphlets under the pseudonym of Peter Porcupine. These have stirred numerous indignant pamphleteers to action, among them one James Quicksilver, the pseudonym adopted by Puglia in order to publish two virulent diatribes against Peter Porcupine and his ilk.[1] *The Blue Shop* and *The Political Massacre*, published in August and September of 1796 respectively, were Puglia's contribution to the violent democratic counter-attack against Cobbett and his conservative ideas. If anything, these pamphlets were every bit as venomous as *El desengaño del hombre*. Puglia clearly reveled at times in letting his own pen run wild as he mounted his caustic assault on Cobbett.

However, James Quicksilver's shortlived venture into pamphleteering ended with *The Political Massacre*, and several years were to pass before any other works from Puglia's pen were to find a printer. Even before he published his attack on despotism, Puglia had been laboring on several other works of various kinds, but of the six unfinished manuscripts he lists at the end of *El desengaño del hombre*, only one, *La pena capital*, was, as we shall see, ultimately destined to see the light of day.[2]

In the meantime Puglia's personal life as distinguished from his literary career is difficult to trace. He appears for the first time in a Philadelphia city directory in 1793, and in subsequent editions of various directories his name reappears from time to time, with innumerable changes of addresses, until it is listed for the last time in the volume for the year 1830 published by Robert Desilver. At that late date his profession is listed merely as interpreter. In several directories he is listed as a "sworn interpreter of foreign languages" (e. g., Robinson's directory for 1816 and Dawe's directory for 1817) and on some occasions his profession is given as "professor of languages"

---

[1] Although Puglia does not overtly identify himself as James Quicksilver in the two pamphlets, there are so many allusions to the author's personal life and his physical appearance that Philadelphia readers must have been aware of his identity. A quarter of a century later Puglia openly claims authorship of the pamphlets in the lists of works published that he appends to *El derecho del hombre, Sistema político-moral de Santiago F. Puglia*, and *Forgery Defeated* (see below, pp. 51-52, 59-60).

[2] See below, pp. 52, 62-63.

(e. g., Desilver's directories for 1823 and 1824). So it is clear that teaching and interpreting foreign languages remained throughout his lifetime among Puglia's most important means of earning a living; and occasionally, as he had before he published *El desengaño del hombre*, he held *official* commissions as interpreter of foreign languages for the commonwealth of Pennsylvania.[3]

In the spring of 1794, presumably just after the publication of *El desengaño del hombre* had freed him to engage once again in gainful employment, Puglia applied for some kind of governmental job in the Department of State and was turned down by Secretary Randolph, apparently with a comment to the effect that *strangers* should not be employed in federal offices. This discrimination against foreign-born citizens angered Puglia and he put his protest in print:

> It is certain that he [i. e., Puglia] is an Italian born, but neither the American laws nor any person acquainted with them, could look upon him as a Stranger, but as a Citizen and an adopted son; the said Gentleman, however, took him for such, perhaps on account of the applicant not being naturally conversant with the *British* dialect.[4]

The reader wonders whether the last line means that Puglia's spoken English was marred by an Italian accent.

Personal and intimate details about Puglia's life and character, save those which he himself chooses to reveal to his readers in his books, are, however, difficult to come by. That he did not marry until he was at least thirty-six years old is to be deduced from the comments, sometimes wry and humorous ones, about his state of bachelorhood that appear in *El desengaño del hombre*[5] and as late as *The Political Massacre*, written in September, 1796, where he refers to himself as a "good-natured batchelor."[6] On one page of *The Blue Shop* he writes of being an old bachelor and also mentions his bald pate.[7] But at some time between 1796 and 1822, when he published *Forgery De-*

---

[3] On October 19, 1796, he was reappointed to this post by Governor Thomas Mifflin (see *Pennsylvania Archives*, 9th Series, II, 1180) and on August 18, 1800, Mifflin's successor, Governor Thomas McKean renewed the appointment (Ibid., III, 1666).
[4] *The Federal Politician*, p. 153.
[5] See above, pp. 36-37.
[6] *The Political Massacre*, p. vi.
[7] *The Blue Shop*, p. vi.

feated, Puglia found himself a wife, for in a footnote to this work, wherein he gives instructions for the disposal of his unpublished manuscripts in the event of his death, Puglia states that "I bequeath them to my beloved wife, heirs, successors, &...." [8] This is the only time that Puglia ever mentions a spouse in any of the documents I have uncovered, nor does he ever make explicit reference to any children save for the vague and unsatisfying line just quoted about "heirs and successors."

It is entirely possible that Puglia's marriage was delayed until quite late in his life; in fact it may not have occurred until after he returned to the United States on April 5, 1808, from a long voyage of thirty-nine months that took him around the world. The only time Puglia mentions this mysterious adventure is in a letter to President Thomas Jefferson wherein he laments the fact that the trade embargo, instituted by Jefferson's administration in December, 1807, has thwarted some of his personal plans. He is careful to assure the President, however, that he approves of his drastic measure despite its adverse effects upon his own fortunes. [9] It is most probable that Puglia's project, which he presumably was planning when he sailed around the world, involved some kind of commercial venture having to do with his old area of expertise, foreign trade.

It appears that when Puglia left Pennsylvania for his trip around the world, he was living in Harrisburg, not Philadelphia. After having been listed in the Philadelphia city directories for 1799, 1800, and 1801, his name disappears for several years; and while I have been unable to discover when he moved or why he went to Harrisburg, he seems to have reached that city by late 1802 and was still residing there in February, 1805. The evidence comes from a minor libel suit in which Puglia was cast in the role of defendant. Seven years after the event he himself tells his side of the story in a footnote to his newspaper articles entitled "On Capital Punishment" wherein he states that the suit was brought against him on December 11, 1802, for having written that the plaintiff, "an unworthy character," was a "liar, imposter and villain." Having come to trial finally on June

---

[8] *Forgery Defeated,* p. 26. By the time of Puglia's death his wife was apparently no longer in the picture. She seems not to have been mentioned in his will. See below, p. 71.

[9] Letter dated Philadelphia, June 21, 1808. See Sowerby, *Catalogue of the Library of Thomas Jefferson,* IV, 557.

16, 1804, the case dragged on, Puglia tells us, until he was in the end fined twenty dollars, though he recalls with considerable satisfaction that Governor Snyder immediately ordered the fine remitted. This occurred in March of 1805.[10]

The whole episode is intriguing. In none of the lists of his published works that he appended to several books published in the 1820's does Puglia make any mention whatsoever of the publication that caused his troubles in Harrisburg, nor indeed does he list any kind of published work between 1796, when *The Political Massacre* appeared, and 1809, when "On Capital Punishment" was printed in *The Democratic Press*. There surely is more to be learned about Puglia's life in Harrisburg, and a search through the public records and newspapers of Dauphin County might reveal what he was doing in the years immediately preceding his trip around the world which began in August or September, 1805.[11]

If at age forty-eight Puglia apparently saw his hopes for a lucrative commercial venture go glimmering because of Jefferson's trade embargo, at forty-nine he finally obtained what seems to have been the first and only long-term job of his entire life. On June 5, 1809, he was commissioned Health Officer of the city of Philadelphia by Governor Simon Snyder,[12] and he held this post until January 21, 1817, when Snyder accepted his resignation.[13] During the eight years covered by this appointment, the erstwhile author apparently published nothing, and, indeed, except for his work as Health Officer,

---

[10] "On Capital Punishment," *The Democratic Press*, January 25, 1811. That the fine was remitted in March, 1805, is confirmed in the Executive Minutes of Governor Thomas McKean (*Pennsylvania Archives, Ninth Series*, III, 2108). Puglia himself provides corroborating evidence that he was still in Harrisburg on February 28, 1805, when he recalls many years later that on that date he wrote a letter from that city to Dr. Charles Caldwell, Vice-President of the Pennsylvania Medical Society, in a vain effort to have the Society give its professional judgment concerning a 48-page manuscript he had sent Caldwell entitled "Inquiry into the Original Cause of the Measles ... [etc.]" (*Forgery Defeated*, pp. 27-28).

[11] Puglia says in his letter to Jefferson on June 21, 1808, that his voyage lasted thirty-one months (see note 8 above). The ship on which he sailed, the Maryland, arrived back in New York on April 5, 1808. (See *U. S. Gazette*, April 6, 1808.)

[12] *Pennsylvania Archives, Ninth Series*, IV, 2715.

[13] Ibid., VI, 4621.

the only event in his life that seems to have left any traces at all is another unimportant court suit that occurred in 1815-1816.[14]

I have been unsuccessful in uncovering any data whatsoever about Puglia's personal life between 1817, when he left his post as Health Officer, and 1821-1822, when he reappears on the literary-political scene with a brief spate of books. In none of the Philadelphia city directories published for the years 1818-1822 inclusive does his name appear, though I have no reason at present to think that he had left Philadelphia, since he makes no mention of any trips in the four books that he published in 1821-1822. The omission of his name is probably not significant since the city was becoming much larger and it is likely that the directories were less complete than they had been earlier when the city was smaller. Desilver's directory for the year 1822 still does not list him, but newspaper advertisements beginning in January, 1822, and running steadily through the month of June prove that during those months Puglia was indeed living in Philadelphia and had established an agency for the sale of lottery tickets.[15] When after a lapse of more than five years Puglia's name finally reappears in a Philadelphia directory, Desilver's *Philadelphia Index or Directory for 1823*, his profession is listed simply as "professor of languages." But at this point in his life his writing career was over, at least as far as published works are concerned, and ironically enough his work as a writer *in Spanish* ends as it began with an edition of *El desengaño del hombre*. A look at these late books by Puglia is in order.

---

[14] Puglia failed to pay a reward offered for the arrest and conviction of a thief and the claimant of the reward, one James Ferrill, brought suit against him. Two legal documents about the case are in the manuscript section of the Historical Society of Pennsylvania.

[15] See *U. S. Gazette*, January 15, 1822.

CHAPTER V

PUGLIA'S PUBLICATIONS IN SPANISH IN 1821-1822

Philadelphia after about 1800 was a very different place from the city where Puglia had sought refuge in 1790. If when he arrived he was one of a tiny group of Spanish-speaking residents, by the end of the second decade of the nineteenth century, Philadelphia, though no longer the capital city of the United States, had become a home, or at least a meeting place, for numerous Spaniards and Spanish Americans. Many of the latter were only temporary residents in their role as active conspirators against Spanish rule in America. Among the very first of these after Puglia, Manuel Torres, who had arrived in Philadelphia from New Granada in 1796, had become a very diplomatic but most effective adviser to the many promotors of Spanish American independence who, from time to time, made their way to the United States in order to plan campaigns, purchase arms, and recruit men for military ventures into various parts of Spanish America; and ultimately, only days before his death on July 15, 1822, Torres saw a dream realized when he was received by President Monroe as Chargé d'Affaires of the Republic of Colombia, the first Spanish American country whose independence was recognized by the United States.[1] But Torres was only one of the most able of many Spanish Americans and a lesser number of Spaniards who resided in or passed through Philadelphia, and not a few of both groups wrote books in Spanish (or English) and had them published by Philadelphia printers. Thus Philadelphia became for Spanish and Spanish

---

[1] For a recent article on Torres, see Charles H. Bowman, "Manuel Torres, A Spanish American Patriot in Philadelphia, 1796-1822," *The Pennsylvania Magazine of History* (Philadelphia), XCIV:1 (January, 1970), 26-53.

American expatriates second only to London as a center for their political and literary activities.

Among the earliest of Hispanic visitors in Philadelphia was Francisco de Miranda, who passed through the city during his first trip to the United States in 1783. He was to return in November, 1805, as he was preparing his ill-fated military expedition to the Coro region of Venezuela. Simón Bolívar was also in the city for a short time in late 1806 on his way home from Europe. Spanish diplomats ranging from the liberal-minded economist Valentín de Foronda to the wily Luis de Onís and the aristocratic Marqués de Casa Irujo cut a wide swath politically, socially, and intellectually for several years around the turn of the century; and some, such as José de Jaudenes, Foronda, and Casa Irujo, were invited to membership in the prestigious American Philosophical Society. The Society itself was most energetic in fomenting scientific and cultural interest in both Spain and Spanish America, and the presence of its distinguished Spanish members was no doubt both cause and effect of this phenomenon. [2]

This is not the place to study in detail the various pamphlets and books in Spanish that began to issue from Philadelphia presses as Spaniards and Spanish Americans congregated in the city. Let it suffice merely to point out some of the more notable political works produced on Pennsylvania soil which carried on from where Puglia left off in 1794. An anonymous pamphlet called *Reflexiones sobre el comercio de España con sus colonias en tiempo de guerra* appeared in 1799,[3] and in 1803 Foronda published anonymously a small fifteen-page opus entitled *Sobre lo que debe hacer un príncipe que tenga colonias a gran distancia* wherein he advocated independence for Spain's American colonies. First among the new generation of propagandists to sign his work was the Venezuelan Manuel García de Sena, who published in 1811 the first translation of Tom Paine's *Common Sense* to be offered in Spanish and included in the same volume Spanish versions of the U. S. Constitution and other revolu-

---

[2] For information about literary and cultural ties between the United States and the Hispanic world, see José de Onís, *The United States as Seen by Spanish American Writers (1776-1890)* (New York: Hispanic Institute in the United States, 1952) and Harry Bernstein, *Making an Inter-American Mind* (Gainesville, Florida: University of Florida Press, 1961).

[3] The pamphlet was published in English in 1800. Several historians have suggested that Torres was the author of the work. Bowman, p. 29.

tionary documents.[4] García de Sena also put into Spanish a history of the United States that was to be widely circulated in Spanish America during the independence period.[5] In 1811 José Álvarez de Toledo, former representative of Santo Domingo in the Cortes at Cádiz, published his vehement *Manifiesto ó satisfaccion pundonorosa, á todos los buenos españoles europeos, y á todos los pueblos de la America, por un diputado de las cortes reunidas en Cadiz,*[6] a justification of his personal conduct in seeking exile in Philadelphia and a plea for Spanish Americans to develop federalist systems of government like that of the United States. In 1812 Álvarez de Toledo was obliged also to issue a defense of his earlier work[7] against a literary attack published in Charleston, South Carolina. Important too in these early years are a *Manual de un republicano para el uso de un pueblo libre,* which appeared anonymously in 1812;[8] Manuel Torres' book published in English in 1816, *An Exposition of the Commerce of Spanish America, with Some Observations upon Its Importance to the United States,* a kind of commercial handbook for North American merchants desirous of doing business in Spanish America; and Luis de Onís' explanation in English of Spanish governmental policies entitled *Observations on the Existing Differences between the Government of Spain and the United States* (1817). In the same year the Venezuelan Juan Germán Roscio published his very influential *El triunfo de la libertad sobre el despotismo, o la confesion de un pecador arrepentido de sus errores politicos, y dedicado a desagraviar, en*

---

[4] *La independencia de la Costa firme justificada por T. Paine treinta años ha. Extracto de sus Obras traducido del inglés al Español por D. Manuel García de Sena* (Filadelfia: T. y J. Palmer, 1811).

[5] *Historia concisa de los Estados Unidos desde el descubrimiento de la América hasta el año de 1807* (Filadelfia: T. y J. Palmer, 1812). The history chosen for translation was that of John M'Culloch, *A Concise History of the United States from the Discovery of America, till 1807.* 3rd edition. Philadelphia: W. M'Culloch, Printer, 1807.

[6] Neither date nor printer is indicated, but the copy owned by the American Philosophical Society is signed in hand by Alvarez de Toledo and dated: Philadelphia, December 10, 1811.

[7] *Contestacion a la carta del Indio Patriota con algunas reflexiones sobre el Diálogo entre el Entusiasta Liberal y el Filósofo Rancio, y sobre las notas anónimas con que ha salido reimpreso el manifiesto de Don José A. de Toledo* (Philadelphia: J. Blocquerst, 1812).

[8] Philadelphia: T. y J. Palmer.

esta parte a la religion ofendida con el sistema de la tiranía,[9] a work designed to convince Spanish American readers that republicanism was not incompatible with traditional Catholic teachings. During a residence in Philadelphia while working as an agent for anti-Iturbide Mexicans, Vicente Rocafuerte, an Ecuadorean admirer of the United States and a man destined to be a reform-minded president of his own country, produced two important statements of his republican political doctrines, *Ideas necesarias a todo pueblo americano independiente, que quiera ser libre*, in 1821,[10] and *Bosquejo ligerísimo de la revolución de Méjico desde el Grito de Iturbide*, in 1822.[11] Equally republican and even more vehement in expressing his views was Father José Servando Teresa de Mier Noriega y Guerra, the flamboyant Mexican veteran of many literary and political battles in London and of military actions ranging from the Napoleonic wars in Spain to the ill-fated Mina expedition to Mexico in 1817, who published his trenchant *Memoria político-instructiva enviada desde Filadelfia en agosto de 1821, a los jefes independientes del Anáhuac, llamado por los españoles Nueva España* (1821),[12] and also en edition of Las Casas' *Breve relación de la destrucción de las Indias occidentales* (1821).[13] Notable too among these writer-politicans was the mercurial Peruvian, Manuel Vidaurre, whose *Cartas americanas*[14] and *Plan del Perú*[15] appeared in Philadelphia in 1823.

This quick resumé includes, of course, only a few of the most notable of some thirty or forty books in Spanish or about Spain or Spanish America that Philadelphia printers published within a space of some twenty years. It is evident, however, even from this partial survey, that politico-literary activity and revolutionary fever were indeed high among Spanish-speaking residents of Philadelphia during

---

[9] Filadelfia: Thomas H. Palmer, 1817.
[10] Philadelphia: D. Huntington, 1821.
[11] Philadelphia: Teracrouef & Naroajeb, 1822.
[12] Philadelphia: J. F. Hurtel, 1821. The book was published anonymously and bibliographers have often mistakenly attributed its authorship to Rocafuerte.
[13] Filadelfia: Juan F. Hurtel, 1821.
[14] *Cartas americanas, políticas y morales, que contienen muchas reflecciones sobre la guerra civil de las Américas*, 2 vols. (Filadelfia: Juan Hurtel, 1823).
[15] *Plan del Perú, defectos del gobierno español antiguo, necesarias reformas* (Philadelphia: J. F. Hurtel, 1823).

the second and third decades of the nineteenth century — what a contrast the aging Puglia must have noted between the 1820's and the ambience of 1794 when his had been a lonely voice crying in the wilderness — and it was only natural that the eldest writer-conspirator of them all should enter the lists once more against his old enemy, Spanish despotism. I have uncovered not one shred of evidence thus far that Puglia moved actively in Spanish American revolutionary circles at this time — no evidence even that he knew Manuel Torres — but his printers were the printers of some of the books penned by the Spanish American revolutionaries, so it is all but inconceivable that he did not cross paths frequently with the younger rebels; though it is also likely, I suspect, that the eccentric old democrat and precursor of their own ideas, now in his sixties, had only limited rapport with a whole new generation of more youthful purveyors of radical thought. Nevertheless, his pen was still active, and he published in the space of a couple of years no fewer than three books in Spanish on political questions: *Sistema político-moral de Santiago Felipe Puglia... Seguido por su traducción de la Lei natural; ó Catequismo del ciudadano francés; obra de C.-F. Volney*, in 1821; [16] a translation of a large part of Paine's *Rights of Man* with the title of *El derecho del hombre*, also in 1821; [17] and a new edition of *El desengaño del hombre*, in 1822. [18] Even while fighting a personal battle against poverty, which he complains of frequently, the sexagenarian warrior found strength to propound once again his long-standing democratic principles to the new reading public created in Spanish America by the increasingly numerous and successful movements toward independence.

In his introductory note to the reader of *El derecho del hombre*, Puglia observes that "... la Obra actual (yá noticiada por mí [in *El desengaño del hombre*] habiendo hecho un efecto admirable al tiempo de su publicación, no puede á menos de hacer lo propio en la época presente," [19] thus taking notice of the politically propitious moment for a study of Paine's ideas by Spanish Americans; and a few months later, in his *Sistema político-moral*, a reference to the prevailing struggle for Spanish American independence is even more explicit:

---

[16] Filadelfia: M. Carey e Hijos.
[17] See note 22 of Chapter I.
[18] Filadelfia: H. C. Carey e I. Lea, 1822.
[19] Unnumbered page [p. v].

> Luego que mi traduccion del *Derecho del Hombre* salió de la imprenta en julio de este año, varias fueron las noticias políticas que nos llegaron del Continente meridional, cuyas provincias beligerantes en la causa sagrada de libertad é independencia, parecen ya por las vicisitudes de las armas, como por el conflicto de opiniones y sistemas, estar vagando todavía, y sin acierto lisongero, en el piélago voluble de su revolucion. [20]

Though worried because things are not going as well as would be desirable in the countries to the south, Puglia expresses his conviction that "... no hai tanto que temer en lo físico, como en lo moral y político de los asuntos allá pendientes," [21] this being the reason why he has chosen at this juncture in history to set down his own political and moral code for the benefit of Spanish American readers and also to translate Volney's political catechism. He indicates, in fact, that none other than Matthew Carey, printer of the volume, had proposed that he translate Volney's work, having in mind no doubt the active demand for such political literature in the Spanish American book market.

Actually, there is nothing new or surprising in the content of the *Sistema político-moral*, and I shall give the work little attention at this time. It is essentially a brief restatement of Puglia's long-standing enlightenment views on politics, mostly ideas derived from Rousseau and his concept of the social contract, Jeffersonian democratic principles, and the author's own experience in the United States. They are the same basic tenets of democratic idealism that underlay the conception of *El desengaño del hombre* and *The Federal Politician*.

Likewise, the new edition of *El desengaño del hombre*, which came out in 1822, was merely a reprinting of the 1794 text with many corrections of spelling and punctuation but with no significant textual changes and no new introduction or personal commentary by the author. In fact, the most illuminating *Adición*, which covered seventeen pages at the end of the 1794 edition and provided so much important information and so many valuable insights into Puglia's life and psychological processes, has been eliminated entirely, presumably because it was judged by the author or the publisher to be dated and of little interest to readers in 1822.

---

[20] *Sistema*, p. iii.
[21] Ibid., p. iv.

Such were Puglia's final efforts with his pen in the struggle against tyranny. Having been the first writer of Spanish to use Philadelphia as his base of operations in the fight against despotism in the Spanish world, he was also prominent among those who finally brought to a victorious conclusion the selfsame politico-literary war that he had initiated three decades earlier.

Chapter VI

OTHER WORKS IN ENGLISH AND UNPUBLISHED MANUSCRIPTS

Neither Puglia's personal biography nor his bibliography is quite complete. Anxious as he was to change the course of history with his political works — and as a political writer he enjoyed his only literary success — there was in Puglia something of the true eighteenth-century encyclopedist in his desire to know many things and to serve all mankind by sharing his knowledge or applying it to the public good. In pursuit of this goal Puglia wrote not only the published books and pamphlets on political questions that have been treated above but many other works as well, works of the most diverse kinds and genres and not excepting creative literature such as poetry and drama.

Already mentioned in passing were six manuscripts that were in various states of preparation at the time they were inventoried at the end of *El desengaño del hombre*: a work on jurisprudence having to do with the problem of capital punishment, one on the practical scientific and mechanical problem of steering balloons, a theological treatise on the sacrament of penance, a pedagogical work that offered a new method for teaching Spanish, a tragicomedy in Italian verse with music, and one "obra alegre, decente y entretenida" whose literary genre is not specified.[1] Of these only the work on capital pun-

---

[1] At the end of the 1794 edition of *El desengaño del hombre*, Puglia lists the titles of these unfinished manuscripts as "La pena capital," "El globo aerostático," "Discursos sobre el sacramento de la penitencia," "Gramática española o método práctico para los ingleses de aprender con facilidad el idioma castellano," "Vicende del comercio, tragicomedia en verso italiano ó *dramma per* música," and "El Cupido."

ishment was ultimately published in a series of newspaper articles appearing in *The Democratic Press* of Philadelphia in 1809-1811, the first part of which was gathered together and published in a small volume that was circulated among all the legislators of Pennsylvania because in 1809 they were actively considering proposals for abolishing capital punishment. Puglia argued for its abolition.[2] After the second part of this work appeared in *The Democratic Press* in late 1810 and early 1811, Puglia attempted to issue the complete work in book form through public subscription, but he was no more successful on this occasion than he had been in 1793 when his efforts to publish *El desengaño del hombre* by the same means ended in failure.[3]

Never published, but apparently written in 1805 while Puglia was in Harrisburg, was a manuscript entitled "Inquiry into the Original Cause of the Measles, Their Symptoms, Progress and Treatment; with Two New Methods for their Innoculation."[4]

Charles Evans in his *American Bibliography* includes an uncertain entry for a play by Puglia, *The Disappointment, or Peter Porcupine in London: A Comedy in Three Acts*, "printed ? by Moreau de St-Mèry" in Philadelphia in 1797.[5] The recently published *National Index of American Imprints through 1800, The Short Title Evans*, states, however, that no copy of this work has ever been located.[6] The entry is almost surely a bibliographical ghost item. In advertisements at the end of both *The Blue Shop* and *The Political Massacre* a play bearing the title indicated and authored by James Quicksilver is promised shortly, but in the three lists of published works that Puglia appends at the end of his *Sistema politico-moral, El derecho del hombre,* and *Forgery Defeated,* the drama is nowhere mentioned, so it seems safe to assume that it was never printed.

Puglia had high hopes indeed for another three-act comedy entitled *The Embargo*, written in 1808 just after he returned from his

---

[2] "Después que se acabó, en la gaceta referida, la publicación de la primera parte, la hice reimprimir en un cuaderno octavo que dediqué al mencionado governador SNYDER, y cada individuo del cuerpo legislativo de este Estado recibió un egemplar de ella." (*El derecho del hombre*, p. 167.) I have been unable to locate any extant copy of this book.
[3] Ibid., pp. 167-168.
[4] See above footnote 10 in Chapter IV.
[5] Vol. XI, item no. 32731.
[6] Compiled by Clifford K. Shipton and James E. Mooney ([Boston?]: American Antiquarian Society and Barre Publishers, 1969), II, 709.

round-the-world voyage and having as its subject matter the trade embargo imposed by Jefferson's administration. Puglia dedicated the work to President Jefferson, and on June 21, 1808, sent a manuscript copy to him for his personal reaction, undoubtedly with the hope that the President might support his efforts to have the play staged and published. Jefferson answered with a polite letter on June 24 thanking the author for the opportunity to see his manuscript, which he reports he had read with pleasure, but expressing his doubts that the anti-embargoists, who were numerous in the commercial cities, would permit their incivism to be blazoned on the stage. Six months later, on December 19, 1808, Puglia once again wrote to Jefferson about some unsuccessful overtures he had made in order to have *The Embargo* and a second three-act comedy, *The Double Disappointment*, acted and printed. He recounts the refusal of Mr. William Warren, Manager of the theater in Philadelphia, to stage his plays, and observes ruefully that "... the Author of the Disappointment must undergo the fate of being himself completely disappointed."[7] A year or two later, in 1810, the frustrated but tenacious dramatist wrote still another three-act drama, *The Merry Tragedy*, which dealt with a father who killed his own son by mistake, but it too failed to reach the boards.[8] Such were Puglia's ill-fated efforts as a playwright. Apparently no more fortunate was an attempt to write an epic poem in the Portuguese language, the existence of which came to light only when a newspaper account of Puglia's death referred to it.[9]

---

[7] For all of this correspondence between Puglia and Jefferson, see Sowerby, *Catalogue of the Library of Thomas Jefferson*, IV, 557-558. There is no record of a reply by Jefferson to Puglia's letter of December 19. *The Double Disappointment* is apparently not related to the early play about Peter Porcupine in London mentioned above (p. 63). There is further confusion in that the play Puglia mentioned to Jefferson in December of 1808 is apparently the one entitled *The Complete Disappointment* listed in *El derecho del hombre* (p. 166) as an unpublished work *written in 1809* and dedicated to Governor Simon Snyder.

[8] Listed in *El derecho del hombre*, p. 166.

[9] See below, p. 71.

Chapter VII

EPILOGUE

When Puglia prepared his last books for publication in 1822 his years were weighing heavily upon him, and expressions of pride, satisfaction, bitterness, and pessimism all merge in his subjective comments upon his life and the public events he was witnessing. The least important for its intrinsic worth of all his publications in the 1821-1822 period, *Forgery Defeated,* a pamphlet that describes a new system which Puglia had patented to prevent the counterfeiting of money, contains a ten-page "Advertisement" which is as invaluable for revealing its author's state of mind in 1822 as the *Adición* to *El desengaño del hombre* had been three decades earlier.

In an opening paragraph, which begins by Puglia's noting the fact that at age sixty-two he probably has little time left on earth, the author comments briefly upon his literary career, claims authorship of several works that had been published anonymously, and complains bitterly of the treatment he has received from several printers. He recalls once again his life in Cádiz and his financial ruin at the hands of Spanish authorities, mentions a brother who had settled in Mexico, and recounts with pride the story of *El desengaño del hombre,* ". . . the first Spanish production printed in this city, and the first also that declared open war against the tyrant of Spain and the Inquisition."[1] With indignation tempered by vanity he recalls that "With diplomatic solemnity my person was demanded of the Federal Republic, by the Spanish monarch, and finally refused," an apparently exaggerated version of the protests sent by Jaudenes and Viar to Secretary

---

[1] *Forgery Defeated,* p. 22.

of State Randolph, and he dramatizes in lurid terms the alleged frustration of Spanish authorities when this tactic failed:

> That Infernal caucus, then styled by the figure antonomasia, the HOLY OFFICE, being thus disappointed in the anxious expectation of celebrating on my individual the usual AUTO DE FE, fulminated against me the grand excommunication, which was proclaimed from all the pulpits of that monarchy, by its monkish preachers and such like clerical impostors. Nay! those hypocritical ministers of the gospel, solemnly promised, in the name of His Catholic Majesty, thousands of dollars for my person dead or alive, calling upon all orthodox christians, anxious for a peremptory passport to Paradise, to exterminate the sacrilegious monster. But in apite of their anathemas, I have all along weathered the storm, which has almost breathed its last, with the additional satisfaction of beholding all my efforts crowned with success, and myself enabled to comment on my prophecies. [2]

Thirty-five years after his financial ruin in Cádiz, Puglia asserts, he once again tried to obtain justice from Spain when in 1820 a revolutionary change of government in Madrid awakened renewed hope that his just claims might receive a favorable hearing, but his letters addressed to a member of the Spanish Cortes have not even been answered because, he charges, "... shame, avarice and intrigue influenced the new government to turn a deaf ear to my complaints." The motive for this shameless denial of justice, Puglia avers, is easy to find: "It is sufficient among the superstitious Castilians, that a man be excommunicated, to forfeit, *ipso facto,* the indefiesible natural rights to life, property, liberty and justice." [3] As part of this same "inexorable persecution" he has also been thwarted in efforts to find out what has happened to the estate of his brother, Peter James Puglia, a Doctor of Medicine who had died in Mexico a few years earlier in opulent circumstances after having become wealthy in the mining business. "Can this be called justice, equity, humanity, morality, religion, christianity, catholicism?," asks Puglia with indignation; "Is it not a political blasphemy to honour the plundering system of Spain, with the name of government?" [4]

---

[2] Ibid. There seems to be a good deal of exaggeration in Puglia's account of this episode. See above, p. 47.

[3] Ibid, p. 23.

[4] Ibid, pp. 23-24.

EPILOGUE

Allowing his anger to subside, Puglia adopts a loftily stoic tone as he takes leave of his readers forever in melodramatic lines that are, however, not devoid of nobility and pathos:

> For my own part, I solemnly declare that the righteousness of my cause, and not the desire of riches, prompts me thus to expose before the impartial World the injustice of that Nation. Covetousness never entered my heart, particularly since my fatal ruin in 1787. Poor and unfortunate, I have all along relied on a kind Providence by my honest industry. Careful in not creating wants, little satisfies me, and I only feel the smart of my reduced circumstances whenever I behold virtue in distress without the means of relieving it. Long accustomed to dangers, I now dispise them; and openly brave the resentment of unmasked tyranny and hypocrisy.
>
> From the supposition of the present being the last of my publications, I do not deem it improper, upon reviewing my past periods of life, to unfold with freedom and candour the opinion which the experience of this world has persuaded me to adopt, and in so doing, I shall confine my sentiments to what I know to be strictly correct without fear of refutation.
>
> The sole and constant object of all my works, has been the instruction and benefit of mankind. They owe me nothing on that account, having assumed the task as a duty in my passage through life. Whatever be my literary reputation, I reared it on my own ground, without intruding on that of others. Satisfied with my own opinion, let others enjoy theirs, whether coincident or discordant. I never sought the regard of my friends by dissimulation, nor courted popularity by art or intrigue. Truth was ever the guide of my actions, yet having seldom doubted the integrity of others, I have been many times most cruelly imposed upon. Respectful of the laws, and affectionate to the Country which protects me, I strenuously endeavour to fulfil my social duties. All religions command my respect, though many of their tenets, mysteries and forms do not meet with my acquiescence. Pleasing, indeed, would it be if I had no enemies, but no man and particularly a Writer, can expect such an exemption; I hear of course their opposition with patience, and find within myself that justice which they occasionally deny me.
>
> Upon viewing my own existence with that rational light, which sometimes springs above the level of its mortal sphere, I cannot but appeal to the stubborn fact, that I was ushered into this sublunary World without my knowledge and consent; of course I had no choice in the vicissitudes through

which I passed, and as all my adversities were the concurrent results of my birth, the justice of their infliction is attributable to an existence, which it was out of my power to prevent. I wish my reflecting mind had been so modified as to be less affected by this severe dispensation, and yielding to a fate thus mysteriously decreed, I am led to conceive, that it is the system of Nature often to bestow upon organic bodies a prodigal share of sensibility, merely to sharpen their feelings in the conflict of a wretched existence. At any rate, had I witnessed Mankind pursuing the sacred rules and practice of Morality, by revering truth, rewarding virtue, maintaining justice, encouraging talents and assisting indigence, my chagrin through life would have experienced some consolation: but Alas! the opposite scene continually disgusted me. Since my early years, I was doomed to view a World involved in unceasing convulsions, usurpations and wars. I have seen criminals happy, baseness successful, wealth adored, imposture exalted, merit disregarded and lewdness fashionable, while the mantles of superstition, and hypocrisy alternately covered, and sanctified the whole. ¿Can the departure from so corrupt a theatre be attended with any regret? ¡None indeed, at least to the just and virtuous! The end of my days will remove the shocking perspective from my sight, by my return to perfect rest. Death so terrible to guilty affluence and vile ambition, wears a mild aspect to the calm and honest philosopher, accustomed to commiserate and drop a tear over the frailties of his species. After having borne with resignation his full share of afflictions, and conscious that he did not deserve so large a portion, no gloomy apprehensions agonize his expiring moments. [5]

With this and a complete list of both his published works and unpublished manuscripts, Puglia gives his readers "my most affectionate farewell," though not without tucking in at the bottom of the page a curious footnote:

My Will is completely prepared for any occurrence. Though no real estate engrosses its contents; the most important object of the same is the disposal of the MSS. I propose to leave. I bequeath them to my beloved wife, heirs, successors, &c. under twelve peremptory orders, the most prominent of which, are All my unpublished works and memoirs, laying in a well-conditioned portable trunk, locked

---

[5] Ibid, pp. 25-26.

EPILOGUE

and sealed, shall be preserved in a place of security. The sale of said trunk, at a *fixed, unalterable* price, shall be advertised, and if within one year and one day after my desease, it is not bought and paid for, it shall be *effectually* burnt. My said orders are so arranged as to compel their strictest execution. [6]

These things said, Puglia falls silent. He figures in *Desilver's Philadelphia Index or Directory for 1823*, where he is listed as a "professor of languages," a listing that is repeated in the directory for 1824, and again in Desilver's directories for 1828, 1829, and 1830 where he is identified as an "interpreter," but then he disappears never to reappear in the directories. He simply drops out of sight.

A coroner's report in the city of Charleston, South Carolina, however, draws back the curtain of oblivion for a brief moment. On the morning of August 29, 1831, the *Charleston Mercury* and the *Charleston Courier* both printed the following item:

> CORONERS REPORT. — A Jury of Inquest was impannelled on Friday last, the 26th inst. in Market-street to inquire into the cause or causes which led to the death of JACQUES PHILIP PUGLIA, a native of Italy, City of Genoa, aged 71 years, a Citizen of the United States of America since 1790, and a resident of the United States ever since. The Jury after due examination into the particulars, came to the unanimous conclusion that the deceased came to his death by deliberately shooting himself with a musket, so arranged in its application to his mouth, as when discharged, produced instantaneous death, the upper part of the scull being blown off by the discharge.
>
> FRANCIS MICHEL, District Coroner

In some five or six days copies of the Charleston papers arrived in Philadelphia and no fewer than three newspapers, *The Philadelphia Gazette and Daily Advertiser* on September 5 and the *Daily Chronicle* and *Poulson's American Daily Advertiser* on September 6, carried identical accounts of Puglia's death, all apparently copied verbatim from the *Charleston Gazette* of August 29, which I have not been able to examine. There is a tragically poignant note in a reporter's stylized efforts to give some importance and human interest to the

---

[6] Ibid, p. 26.

lonely suicide of a person about whom the writer obviously knew very little. For the reader who has followed me through this account of Puglia's life and career, and particularly for one who has read with understanding the poignant farewell to his reading public that Puglia appended to *Forgery Defeated*, the anonymous reporter's limited information and half truths obviously gleaned from talking to a few people who had known the aged Italian only slightly — he could not have lived in Charleston more than two years — are pregnant with meaning and with high pathos:

> *Remarkable Suicide* — A report of the Coronor and Jury of Inquest, in this morning's *Gazette*, informs us of the death by suicide of Mr. JACQUES PHILIP PUGLIA, an Italian by birth, but for many years a resident of the United States and of this city. Mr. Puglia was a reduced gentleman, of fine attainments, and, it is said, of a mind, naturally strong, active and penetrating.
>
> He had sustained life, and little more, in our city, by teaching the modern languages to a few scholars; but increasing years and necessities, and the difficulties of making the means mete out the ends of life, determined him, deliberately, to commit the rash act, which makes him a felon in the consideration of the law, and subtracts largely from the merits of a life, said otherwise to have been of the most exemplary character. Some recent disappointments, in not obtaining a situation in a literary institution, for which he had applied, precipitated a resolution, in the previous and frequent consideration of which, he had freely and openly indulged. Accordingly, on Friday last, with a musket loaded with shot, he laid himself down, and by a string wrapped round his finger, connected with the trigger, he shot himself through the head, and immediately expired.
>
> Prior to this act, and with a coolness utterly at variance, with the sanity, or, as he probably considered it, the philosophy of the deed, he wrote letters to sundry persons, detailing his reasons for its commission, and speaking of it as indifferently as the most common occurrence. These reasons are such as we have substantially described them, and, however insufficient under the estimate of a truly moral standard, to prove a warrant for suicide, were no doubt sufficiently satisfactory to his mind, for that purpose. His will, which we have read, and which for the absence of some essential formalities, is valueless, after briefly stating, in clear and precise language, his determination — describes his possessions as contained in a single trunk, the measure of which is given.

This trunk he values at $2100. It is stated to contain the manuscripts and correspondence of Mr. P. and he especially enumerates among these, an Epic, in the Portuguese language, which he says, in one part, by a singular accomodation of the material to the matter, affords a precise description of Philadelphia, in which city, he lived for many years.

This trunk, unopened, is to be exposed for sale for a certain period of time, and if disposed of, must bring the valuation of $2100 laid upon it; which sum thus realized, he divides into three equal parts to individual friends. In the event of their finding no purchaser, they are, unopened, to be destroyed by fire.

His body he requires to be buried, in the plainest manner, in a grave eight feet deep, without any designation by "staff or stone" of the spot, and at *midnight*; all of which requisitions, we believe, were punctually complied with.

Mr. Puglia, we have been informed, was an active agitator, many years since, at the Court of Old Spain, and from his talents, which are said to have been of no humble description, exercised against the Government, he became peculiarly obnoxious, and was compelled to fly to our country — a price having been set upon his head. Here he became a kind of Secretary, probably for the purpose of translation, to Mr. Jefferson, and a formal demand of his person is said to have been made upon the administration, by the Court of Spain. It is supposed, that, among the contents of the trunk, upon which he has put this evaluation, there will be found some of the secret history of, and proceedings in relation to the Spanish government; the possession of which rendered him so obnoxious in that quarter. Conversations are remembered by his acquaintances, in which this conjecture finds confirmation.

So ended a life. It was a life with few triumphs and many disappointments, but Puglia undeniably carved out for himself a small but respectable niche in the history of Spanish American independence and of political literature associated with that event, though many details of his passage through life remain in the shadows. Exactly what happened in Cádiz that brought about his financial ruin? Was he perhaps a member of the radical political clubs that flourished in that southern Spanish city in the 1780's? What was he doing in Harrisburg between 1802 and 1805? When did he marry, and what of his home life and his family? Did he have any personal contacts with men like Vicente Rocafuerte, Servando Teresa de Mier, Manuel Vidaurre and the other writer-conspirators who were active in Philadelphia during the second and third decades of the nineteenth century? On the assumption that nobody was ingenuous enough to pay $2100 for a sealed trunk containing a few manuscripts and letters of uncertain value, were Puglia's papers actually destroyed in accordance with the instructions of his will? In short, the questions are legion and answers for many of them remain to be found.

I hope, however, that this modest preliminary study may serve to bring to the fore a worthy precursor of Spanish American independence, one of the very first of many estimable author-politicians who turned their writing talent against Spanish rule in America. Even if, as Miguel Batllori believes, Juan Pablo Viscardo y Guzmán wrote his justly famous *Lettre aux americains-espagnols* before October 12, 1792,[7] and thus was the first writer to wield his pen in the struggle for independence, let it be remembered that he wrote his *Lettre* in French, that it was not published until 1799, and that it did not appear in Spanish translation until 1801. Even Antonio Nariño's translation of the *Droits de l'homme* was published only a few days before *El desengaño del hombre* in late 1793 or early 1794. Furthermore, it appears that Nariño was no more successful than Puglia in seeing his printed work circulate among Spanish American readers.[8] So Puglia's place among the first of many notable propagandists who wrote *in Spanish* to further the cause of democratic ideals and of Spanish American independence is secure. That he was ahead of his time and that circumstances, principally Genet's disastrous career as

---

[7] Miguel Batllori, *El abate Viscardo, historia y mito de la intervención de los jesuitas en la independencia de Hispanoamérica* (Caracas: Instituto Panamericano de Historia y Geografía, 1953), p. 128.

[8] After Nariño was imprisoned in August, 1794, he claimed that the entire edition of one hundred copies of his work, *Discurso sobre los derechos naturales del hombre*, was immediately burned as soon as he realized that Spanish authorities had gotten wind of it. If any copies actually circulated, they have never come to light. None could be found to be used as evidence against Nariño at his trial, and today no copy of the original printing is known. In 1811 Nariño himself made a new printing of the work, but it is not clear whether he once again translated the French text or whether he reprinted his earlier translation working directly from a copy that he had successfully hidden. See Thomas Blossom, *Nariño, Hero of Colombian Independence* (Tucson, Arizona: University of Arizona Press, 1967), pp. 9-21; also Eduardo Posada, *Bibliografía bogotona* (Bogotá: Imprenta de Arboleda y Valencia, 1917), Vol. I, pp. 93 ff.

a diplomat, conspired to prevent *El desengaño del hombre* from having the impact that Puglia was seeking cannot be doubted. The historian of Spanish American independence and of the printed word's role in the struggle cannot help wondering what might have been the effect of Puglia's inflammatory book if Genet had been more successful in his plans to support George Rogers Clark's military incursion against the Spanish in Louisiana and, as a consequence, *El desengaño del hombre* had fallen into the hands of a substantial number of readers in New Spain and the rest of Spanish America. At the very least Viceroy Branciforte and the Inquisitors of New Spain would have spent a few more uneasy days and troubled nights, and it is highly probable that Puglia's place in the political and literary histories of the independence period would have been significantly enhanced.

BIBLIOGRAPHY OF THE WORKS OF SANTIAGO F. PUGLIA

Puglia, James Ph. de. *A Short Extract (Concerning the Rights of Men and Titles) from the Work Entitled Man Undeceived, Written in Spanish by James Ph. de Puglia...* [etc.]. Philadelphia: Printed by Johnston & Justice, 1793. 16 pp.

Puglia, Santiago F. *Desengaño del hombre*. Filadelfia: En la imprenta de Francisco Bailey, 1794. x, 113, xvii pp.

Puglia, James Ph. *The Federal Politician*. Philadelphia: Printed by Francis & Robert Bailey, 1795. xxiii, 284 pp.

Quicksilver, James [pseudonym]. *The Blue Shop or Impartial and Humorous Observations on the Life and Adventures of Peter Porcupine...* [etc.] *by James Quicksilver*. Philadelphia: Printed by Moreau de St-Méry, August, 1796. viii, 52 pp.

Quicksilver, James [pseudonym]. *The Political Massacre, or Unexpected Observations on the Writings of Our Present Scribblers. By James Quicksilver*. Philadelphia: Printed by Moreau de St-Méry, September, 1796. vi, 29 pp.

ME [pseudonym]. "On Capital Punishments." *The Democratic Press* (Philadelphia), April 10, 1809; April 19, 1809; April 28, 1809; May 8, 1809; May 12, 1809; May 20, 1809; June 17, 1809; December 19, 1810; December 20, 1810; December 22, 1810; December 26, 1810; December 28, 1810; December 31, 1810; January 3, 1811; January 9, 1811; January 25, 1811; February 12, 1811.

Puglia, Santiago F., trans. *El derecho del hombre, para el uso y provecho del género humano. Compuesto por don Tomás Paine...* [etc.]. Traducido del inglés por Santiago Felipe Puglia. Filadelfia: De la Imprenta de H. Carey é Hijos, 1821. xi, 168 pp.

Puglia, Santiago Felipe. *Sistema político-moral de Santiago Felipe Puglia. Seguido por su traducción de la Lei natural; ó, Catequismo del ciudadano frances: obra de C.-F. Volney*. Filadelfia: Imprenta de M. Carey é Hijos, 1821. vii, 69, 56 pp.

Puglia, James Ph. *Forgery Defeated; or A New Plan for Invalidating and Detecting All Attempts of the Kind; For Which a Patent Has Been Obtained from the United States*. Philadelphia: J. F. Hurtel, 1822. 30 pp.

Puglia, Santiago F. *El desengaño del hombre*. Filadelfia: H. C. Carey e I. Lea, 1822. 257 pp. [actually 157 pp. because the numbering jumps from 121 to 222]

NORTH CAROLINA STUDIES IN THE ROMANCE LANGUAGES AND LITERATURES

I.S.B.N. Prefix 0-8078-

Recent Titles

PROPER NAMES IN THE LYRICS OF THE TROUBADOURS, by Frank M. Chambers. 1971. (No. 113). -913-8.

STUDIES IN HONOR OF MARIO A. PEI, edited by John Fisher and Paul A. Gaeng. 1971. (No. 114). -914-6.

DON MANUEL CAÑETE, CRONISTA LITERARIO DEL ROMANTICISMO Y DEL POS-ROMANTICISMO EN ESPAÑA, por Donald Allen Randolph. 1972. (No. 115). -915-4.

THE TEACHINGS OF SAINT LOUIS. A CRITICAL TEXT, by David O'Connell. 1972. (No. 116). -916-2.

HIGHER, HIDDEN ORDER: DESIGN AND MEANING IN THE ODES OF MALHERBE, by David Lee Rubin. 1972. (No. 117). -917-0.

JEAN DE LE MOTE "LE PARFAIT DU PAON," édition critique par Richard J. Carey. 1972. (No. 118). -918-9.

CAMUS' HELLENIC SOURCES, by Paul Archambault. 1972. (No. 119). -919-7.

FROM VULGAR LATIN TO OLD PROVENÇAL, by Frede Jensen. 1972. (No. 120). -920-0.

GOLDEN AGE DRAMA IN SPAIN: GENERAL CONSIDERATION AND UNUSUAL FEATURES, by Sturgis E. Leavitt. 1972. (No. 121). -921-9.

THE LEGEND OF THE "SIETE INFANTES DE LARA" (*Refundición toledana de la crónica de 1344* versión), study and edition by Thomas A. Lathrop. 1972. (No. 122). -922-7.

STRUCTURE AND IDEOLOGY IN BOIARDO'S "ORLANDO INNAMORATO," by Andrea di Tommaso. 1972. (No. 123). -923-5.

STUDIES IN HONOR OF ALFRED G. ENGSTROM, edited by Robert T. Cargo and Emmanuel J. Mickel, Jr. 1972. (No. 124). -924-3.

A CRITICAL EDITION WITH INTRODUCTION AND NOTES OF GIL VICENTE'S "FLORESTA DE ENGANOS," by Constantine Christopher Stathatos. 1972. (No. 125). -925-1.

LI ROMANS DE WITASSE LE MOINE. *Roman du treizième siècle.* Édité d'après le manuscrit, fonds français 1553, de la Bibliothèque Nationale, Paris, par Denis Joseph Conlon. 1972. (No. 126). -926-X.

EL CRONISTA PEDRO DE ESCAVIAS. *Una vida del Siglo XV,* por Juan Bautista Avalle-Arce. 1972. (No. 127). -927-8.

AN EDITION OF THE FIRST ITALIAN TRANSLATION OF THE "CELESTINA," by Kathleen V. Kish. 1973. (No. 128). -928-6.

MOLIÈRE MOCKED. THREE CONTEMPORARY HOSTILE COMEDIES: *Zélinde, Le portrait du peintre, Élomire Hypocondre,* by Frederick Wright Vogler. 1973. (No. 129). -929-4.

C.-A. SAINTE-BEUVE. *Chateaubriand et son groupe littéraire sous l'empire.* Index alphabétique et analytique établi par Lorin A. Uffenbeck. 1973. (No. 130). -930-8.

THE ORIGINS OF THE BAROQUE CONCEPT OF "PEREGRINATIO," by Juergen Hahn. 1973. (No. 131). -931-6.

THE "AUTO SACRAMENTAL" AND THE PARABLE IN SPANISH GOLDEN AGE LITERATURE, by Donald Thaddeus Dietz. 1973. (No. 132). -932-4.

FRANCISCO DE OSUNA AND THE SPIRIT OF THE LETTER, by Laura Calvert. 1973. (No. 133). -933-2.

When ordering please cite the *ISBN Prefix* plus the last four digits for each title.

Send orders to: University of North Carolina Press
Chapel Hill
North Carolina 27514
U. S. A.

NORTH CAROLINA STUDIES IN THE ROMANCE LANGUAGES AND LITERATURES

I.S.B.N. Prefix 0-8078-

Recent Titles

ITINERARIO DI AMORE: DIALETTICA DI AMORE E MORTE NELLA VITA NUOVA, by Margherita de Bonfils Templer. 1973. (No. 134). -934-0.
L'IMAGINATION POETIQUE CHEZ DU BARTAS: ELEMENTS DE SENSIBILITE BAROQUE DANS LA "CREATION DU MONDE," by Bruno Braunrot. 1973. (No. 135). -934-0.
ARTUS DESIRE: PRIEST AND PAMPHLETEER OF THE SIXTEENTH CENTURY, by Frank S. Giese. 1973. (No. 136). -936-7.
JARDIN DE NOBLES DONZELLAS, FRAY MARTIN DE CORDOBA, by Harriet Goldberg. 1974. (No. 137). -937-5.
MYTHE ET PSYCHOLOGIE CHEZ MARIE DE FRANCE DANS "GUIGEMAR", par Antoinette Knapton. 1975. (No. 142). -942-1.
THE LYRIC POEMS OF JEHAN FROISSART: A CRITICAL EDITION, by Rob Roy McGregor, Jr. 1975. (No. 143). -943-X.
THE HISPANO-PORTUGUESE CANCIONERO OF THE HISPANIC SOCIETY OF AMERICA, by Arthur Askins. 1974. (No. 144). -944-8.
HISTORIA Y BIBLIOGRAFÍA DE LA CRÍTICA SOBRE EL "POEMA DE MÍO CID" (1750-1971), por Miguel Magnotta. 1976. (No. 145). -945-6.
LES ENCHANTEMENZ DE BRETAIGNE. AN EXTRACT FROM A THIRTEENTH CENTURY PROSE ROMANCE "LA SUITE DU MERLIN", edited by Patrick C. Smith. 1977. (No. 146). -9146-0.
THE DRAMATIC WORKS OF ÁLVARO CUBILLO DE ARAGÓN, by Shirley B. Whitaker. 1975. (No. 149). -949-9.
A CONCORDANCE TO THE "ROMAN DE LA ROSE" OF GUILLAUME DE LORRIS, by Joseph R. Danos. 1976. (No. 156). 0-88438-403-9.
POETRY AND ANTIPOETRY: A STUDY OF SELECTED ASPECTS OF MAX JACOB'S POETIC STYLE, by Annette Thau. 1976. (No. 158). -005-X.
FRANCIS PETRARCH, SIX CENTURIES LATER, by Aldo Scaglione. 1975. (No. 159).
STYLE AND STRUCTURE IN GRACIÁN'S "EL CRITICÓN", by Marcia L. Welles, 1976. (No. 160). -007-6.
MOLIERE: TRADITIONS IN CRITICISM, by Laurence Romero. 1974 (Essays, No. 1). -001-7.
CHRÉTIEN'S JEWISH GRAIL. A NEW INVESTIGATION OF THE IMAGERY AND SIGNIFICANCE OF CHRÉTIEN DE TROYES'S GRAIL EPISODE BASED UPON MEDIEVAL HEBRAIC SOURCES, by Eugene J. Weinraub. 1976. (Essays, No. 2). -002-5.
STUDIES IN TIRSO, I, by Ruth Lee Kennedy. 1974. (Essays, No. 3). -003-3.
VOLTAIRE AND THE FRENCH ACADEMY, by Karlis Racevskis. 1975. (Essays, No. 4). -004-1.
THE NOVELS OF MME RICCOBONI, by Joan Hinde Stewart. 1976. (Essays, No. 8). -008-4.
FIRE AND ICE: THE POETRY OF XAVIER VILLAURRUTIA, by Merlin H. Forster. 1976. (Essays, No. 11). -011-4.
THE THEATER OF ARTHUR ADAMOV, by John J. McCann. 1975. (Essays, No. 13). -013-0.
AN ANATOMY OF POESIS: THE PROSE POEMS OF STÉPHANE MALLARMÉ, by Ursula Franklin. 1976. (Essays, No. 16). -016-5.
LAS MEMORIAS DE GONZALO FERNÁNDEZ DE OVIEDO, Vols. I and II, by Juan Bautista Avalle-Arce. 1974. (Texts, Textual Studies, and Translations, Nos. 1 and 2). -401-2; 402-0.
GIACOMO LEOPARDI: THE WAR OF THE MICE AND THE CRABS, translated, introduced and annotated by Ernesto G. Caserta. 1976. (Texts, Textual Studies, and Translations, No. 4). -404-7.

When ordering please cite the *ISBN Prefix* plus the last four digits for each title.

Send orders to: University of North Carolina Press
  Chapel Hill
  North Carolina 27514
  U. S. A.

NORTH CAROLINA STUDIES IN THE ROMANCE LANGUAGES AND LITERATURES

I.S.B.N. Prefix 0-8078-

Recent Titles

LUIS VÉLEZ DE GUEVARA: A CRITICAL BIBLIOGRAPHY, by Mary G. Hauer. 1975. (Texts, Textual Studies, and Translations, No. 5). -405-5.

UN TRÍPTICO DEL PERÚ VIRREINAL: "EL VIRREY AMAT, EL MARQUÉS DE SOTO FLORIDO Y LA PERRICHOLI". EL "DRAMA DE DOS PALANGANAS" Y SU CIRCUNSTANCIA, estudio preliminar, reedición y notas por Guillermo Lohmann Villena. 1976. (Texts, Textual Studies, and Translation, No. 15). -415-2.

LOS NARRADORES HISPANOAMERICANOS DE HOY, edited by Juan Bautista Avalle-Arce. 1973. (Symposia, No. 1). -951-0.

ESTUDIOS DE LITERATURA HISPANOAMERICANA EN HONOR A JOSÉ J. ARROM, edited by Andrew P. Debicki and Enrique Pupo-Walker. 1975. (Symposia, No. 2). -952-9.

MEDIEVAL MANUSCRIPTS AND TEXTUAL CRITICISM, edited by Christopher Kleinhenz. 1976. (Symposia, No. 4). -954-5.

SAMUEL BECKETT. THE ART OF RHETORIC, edited by Edouard Morot-Sir, Howard Harper, and Dougald McMillan III. 1976. (Symposia, No. 5). -955-3.

DELIE. CONCORDANCE, by Jerry Nash. 1976. 2 Volumes. (No. 174).

FIGURES OF REPETITION IN THE OLD PROVENÇAL LYRIC: A STUDY IN THE STYLE OF THE TROUBADOURS, by Nathaniel B. Smith. 1976. (No. 176). -9176-2.

A CRITICAL EDITION OF LE REGIME TRESUTILE ET TRESPROUFITABLE POUR CONSERVER ET GARDER LA SANTE DU CORPS HUMAIN, by Patricia Willett Cummins. 1977. (No. 177).

THE DRAMA OF SELF IN GUILLAUME APOLLINAIRE'S "ALCOOLS", by Richard Howard Stamelman. 1976. (No. 178). -9178-9.

A CRITICAL EDITION OF "LA PASSION NOSTRE SEIGNEUR" FROM MANUSCRIPT 1131 FROM THE BIBLIOTHEQUE SAINTE-GENEVIEVE, PARIS, by Edward J. Gallagher. 1976. (No. 179). -9179-7.

A QUANTITATIVE AND COMPARATIVE STUDY OF THE VOCALISM OF THE LATIN INSCRIPTIONS OF NORTH AFRICA, BRITAIN, DALMATIA, AND THE BALKANS, by Stephen William Omeltchenko. 1977. (No. 180). -9180-0.

OCTAVIEN DE SAINT-GELAIS "LE SEJOUR D'HONNEUR", edited by Joseph A. James. 1977. (No. 181). -9181-9.

A STUDY OF NOMINAL INFLECTION IN LATIN INSCRIPTIONS, by Paul A. Gaeng. 1977. (No. 182). -9182-7.

THE LIFE AND WORKS OF LUIS CARLOS LÓPEZ, by Martha S. Bazik. 1977. (No. 183). -9183-5.

LANGUAGE IN GIOVANNI VERGA'S EARLY NOVELS, by Nicholas Patruno. 1977. (No. 188). -9188-6.

BLAS DE OTERO EN SU POESÍA, by Moraima de Semprún Donahue. 1977. (No. 189). -9189-4.

LA ANATOMÍA DE "EL DIABLO COJUELO": DESLINDES DEL GÉNERO ANATOMÍSTICO, por C. George Peale. 1977. (No. 191). -9191-6.

MONTAIGNE AND FEMINISM, by Cecile Insdorf. 1977. (No. 194). -9194-0.

SANTIAGO F. PUGLIA, AN EARLY PHILADELPHIA PROPAGANDIST FOR SPANISH AMERICAN INDEPENDENCE, by Merle S. Simmons. 1977. (No. 195). -9195-9.

When ordering please cite the *ISBN Prefix* plus the last four digits for each title.

Send orders to: University of North Carolina Press
                  Chapel Hill
                  North Carolina 27514
                  U. S. A.

The Department of Romance Studies Digital Arts and Collaboration Lab at the University of North Carolina at Chapel Hill is proud to support the digitization of the North Carolina Studies in the Romance Languages and Literatures series.

www.ingramcontent.com/pod-product-compliance
Lightning Source LLC
Chambersburg PA
CBHW020422230426
43663CB00007BA/1272